Africanizing Christian Art

For Sue, beloved spouse, colleague, and inspiration

CONTENTS

ILLUSTRATIONS

A LINE FROM THE PROVINCIAL

I am delighted to be associated with Nick Bridger's book on the late Father Kevin Carroll, SMA, and the Oye-Ekiti scheme. Having served for some months in 1979 as priest in charge of Oye-Ekiti parish, I find this book of even greater personal interest.

Since becoming involved in this production, I have admired Nick's enthusiasm for his subject and his determination and perseverance to see it through to the end. It has involved years of research and writing; it has also required considerable patience to bring it to completion.

Through this work, Nick is doing a real service to the Society of African Missions (SMA). Father Carroll's work has not always been as fully appreciated by his confreres in the Society as it might have been. Is it a case of the prophet not being accepted in his own country? Though he did inspire some members to appreciate this way of inculturating the Gospel, it would also be true to say that he has had no real disciples in succeeding generations. Much of what Nick uncovers in this book will be eye opening for many SMA members. The depth of Father Carroll's understanding of the place of indigenous art in communicating the Gospel should inspire us to look again at his legacy and see where we might profitably use this knowledge in the work of evangelization today.

I had always thought that Father Carroll was perhaps too far ahead of his time to gain the appreciation of his contemporaries. Yet it was revealing to learn that he had the support of Cardinal Celso Costantini, a well-placed figure at the Vatican. With such backing, one might have expected Father Carroll's work to have had a greater impact.

I believe this book will go a long way toward reclaiming the gift that Kevin Carroll was to the Society and to mission. One can now seriously hope that his original and magisterial contribution to mission will have a deeper impact on those who succeed him, perhaps especially among the indigenous African members of our Society.

I applaud Nick for this excellent production. I trust that you will find it both engaging and inspiring.

Fachtna O'Driscoll, SMA
Provincial Leader, Irish Province

FOREWORD

Art, Palm Wine, and Margarine:
Journeys with Father Kevin

Father Kevin Carroll, SMA, was first and foremost a dedicated Catholic priest, living a life utterly true to that vocation. He was brought up and trained within the Tridentine tradition, which was normal then if controversial now. Traveling together in Nigeria in the early 1960s, researching local arts, we would camp for the night in a village church, and I would serve his Mass first thing the next morning. In his work on the project of inculturation, a substantial part of which is described in this much-needed book, he might have seemed a revolutionary, yet he often told me, "I always work within the rules: then no one can complain!" The Missal, the Breviary, the rules of his missionary order, obedience to his superiors—these were the basis of everything he accomplished.

It so happens, though none of us had realized it until Nick Bridger's research, that the Oye-Ekiti project was fully in conformity with insights developed within Catholic Christianity through the previous hundred years by Bishop Melchior de Marion Brésillac (1800–56), founder of the Society of African Missions; within the Vatican by Cardinal Celso Costantini (1877–1958), head of Propaganda Fide; and then in Nigeria, under the guidance of the Reverend Dr. Patrick Kelly (1904–88), Father Kevin's immediate superior. It is one of those profoundly sad ironies that there would be those among both clergy and laity in Nigeria who would find these developments not to their liking! We should all be grateful, therefore, to Nick Bridger for setting the record straight in these matters. His research across three continents has identified many of the works coming from the Oye-Ekiti project that otherwise would have remained forgotten, their place in the histories of an African Christian art unknown, and indeed the very existence of an African Christian art ignored.

Not least among Father Kevin's qualities was the gift of tongues. His knowledge of languages was the very foundation of all his work in the arts, his pioneering development in the material culture of Catholic Christianity in Nigeria, and his encouragement of Yoruba-language poetic texts and musical forms. He could converse directly with artists, poets, and musicians. He was fluent in the Yoruba language, albeit spoken (as I recall) with a Scouse accent, and his complete command of Yoruba also gave him a sound basis for the critical judgment of academic research. He was, for example, able to say of the author of a pioneering book on Yoruba drumming and its analysis of the relationship between musical and spoken-language tone that "the problem . . . is that he does not understand Yoruba, and how the tones change in particular grammatical circumstances!" Of another scholar who had muddled the tones of two quite different concepts, he wrote to me: "It has shaken my confidence in him considerably." This could be mistaken for mere pedantry, when in reality he was deeply concerned about the extraordinary difficulties of translating key terms and concepts. In due course, that command of Yoruba also facilitated his studies of Hausa and other Nigerian languages.

Father Kevin was, however, no idealizing traditionalist looking back to a nostalgic what-might-have-been world; his intentions were never the reinvention of a now-Catholic Yoruba Christianity derived from a village-based farming culture. He was a modernizer, and he was well read in current developments in Catholic art and architecture. (I still treasure the copy of *Contemporary Church Art*, published in 1956 by Sheed and Ward, that he gave me.) He had the sure knack of knowing what would work with a contemporary Nigerian audience. Moreover, his interests in the visual arts ranged across every medium—sculpture, painting, printmaking, textile design, architecture, cast brass, wrought ironwork—and every period, from the traditions of antiquity and the recent past to modernist and contemporary popular developments. He was also himself an artist. Does anyone know what has happened to the magnificent triptych he painted for the University of Ibadan chapel (see Carroll 1958)?

Though best known for his work with sculptors Areogun, George Bandele Areogun, and Lamidi Olonade Fakeye, Father Carroll also worked with painter and printmaker Bruce Onobrakpeya as well as a great many other artists who were graduates of a developing university fine-art program in Nigeria, in contrast to the workshop/apprenticeship tradition that was the foundation of the Oye-Ekiti project. Onobrakpeya was neither Yoruba nor Catholic, but had evolved a figurative and decorative style that made use of older forms of art, in effect bringing them into a modern world that had transcended the limitations of ethnicity, and his magnificent Stations of the Cross in St. Paul's Church, Ebute-Metta (sadly now in a very decayed condition and in urgent need of conservation and restoration), is perhaps the greatest monument to a developing Nigerian art in which the Catholic Church has a particularly honorable place. (In this context, it is worth noting that in apartheid South Africa in the 1960s, black artists enjoyed Catholic Church patronage [see Miles 2004, 49–70].) Onobrakpeya was thereby able to develop a Nigerian patronage sufficient to allow him to quit his post at St. Gregory's and maintain himself as an independent artist. Of the work of another expatriate cultural entrepreneur in Nigeria, Father Kevin once said, "When Nigerians are prepared to put money into that art, I'll believe in it!" He was therefore justifiably gratified by the eventual success of the Oye-Ekiti project. I received a letter from him dated January 1969 in which he remarks, "I write from Osi-Ilorin [Areogun's and George Bandele's home village] where there has been a carving explosion among young men," and by the 1980s, he reckoned that at least twenty-five sculptors had come out of the Oye-Ekiti project and were working in Nigeria, having built up their own patronage. In addition, Lamidi was employed by the university art department at Ife, and George Bandele's son Gabriel held a similar position at Zaria.

Father Kevin was an unassuming and completely unpretentious man. He taught me how to do field research and about the refreshing delights of palm wine. I also learned from him that I should take an interest in all aspects of and developments in Nigerian art practice if I were to have any hope of understanding anything. It was no use privileging one genre or medium over another. I had arrived in Nigeria in 1961 in my twenty-third year to work for the Federal Department of Antiquities at the Lagos Museum. I'd spent a few months at the British Museum, where I learned something of Nigerian art from the great pioneer of African art studies William Fagg, whose younger brother, Bernard, was then director of antiquities in Nigeria. The Faggs were Catholic and friends of Father Kevin's, and they were my introduction to him. I had been received into the Church two years previously, at the end of my undergraduate studies in anthropology, but I had no idea how to do the research my studies required.

Father Kevin was also something of an ascetic. I remember visiting him at the mission at Ijebu-Igbo when his confreres were away, and dinner was just spaghetti and margarine (and cold beer, so it can't have been Lent). At best, one could say that, aside from the arts (and the occasional draft of palm wine in a Yoruba village), he had no interest in the pleasures and comforts of this world. He was, however, devoted to Africa, and in his last letter, in December 1992, when he was in his seventy-third year, the same age as I am now, he had written to Sue and me, "Please God I will have a few more years in Africa, or even have a perpetual residence permit for my old bones." That wish was granted sooner than any of us had expected. He is buried in Ibadan, and we still miss him.

Father Kevin Carroll was a legendary figure from whom we all still have much to learn. I'd like to think that Nick Bridger's well-researched book is just the beginning of that process. There is, after all, so much more work still to be done on the forms of inculturation, their realization in the visual arts, and their reception in Nigeria and throughout Africa. The histories of a modern Christian art in sub-Saharan Africa remain an exciting and still almost completely unresearched field of study. Nick Bridger's book is the exception, and, as such, it provides the model for further research.

However, notwithstanding my personal memories of, and my intellectual and practical debts to, a much-loved priest, this book was never intended to be read as biography. It is, rather, the history of a new genre of art within the context of a modern Nigeria, and it is the first comprehensive study of the engagement between the iconographical demands of Catholic Christianity and a particular, local sculptural tradition in sub-Saharan Africa. It opens up the very recognition that there is such a thing, and it celebrates the prophetic insights of Bishop Brésillac, Cardinal Costantini, and Father Kelly, who believed it would lead to an art worthy of research, publication, and exhibition. For this book, published by the Irish Province of the Society of African Missions, to which Father Kevin belonged, also provides the basis for the first comprehensive exhibition of the work he was able to draw out of the artists working with the Oye-Ekiti project. The exhibition is sponsored by the Irish Province of the Society of African Missions. We all owe Nick Bridger our profound thanks for moving us beyond reminiscence and anecdote and, through his research and in this publication, recovering forgotten insights and neglected works of art, thereby giving us the first study of a hitherto overlooked field in the anthropology and history of art in sub-Saharan Africa.

John Picton
Emeritus Professor of African Art,
School of Oriental and African Studies,
University of London

JOHN PICTON is Emeritus Professor of African Art, School of Oriental and African Studies, University of London, where he worked from 1979 to 2003. He was employed by the Nigerian Government Department of Antiquities (1961–70) and the British Museum (1970–79). He, his wife, Sue, and their daughter, Josephine, and son, Matthew, live in Evesham, Worcestershire.

PREFACE

Why write a cross-disciplinary, illustrated book on a rarely seen, little-known Nigerian religious art genre? My motives originated in an art history teacher's desire to present students with fascinating and innovative subject matter. My acquaintance with this topic began in 2000, when I was looking for a possible graduate thesis topic. After decades of teaching history and anthropology in the classroom, I responded to a midlife urge for change and decided to try something new, the legal profession. Later, after a brief sojourn in law school and practice, I found I still missed the interaction with students, the discussions of interesting subject matter, and the pursuit of scholarly learning, all part of the academic life. Shifting my focus to world art history seemed like a good way to revitalize a return to teaching in my fifties.

Stimulated by trips to Asia and, particularly, Africa, under the auspices of the Research Expeditions Programs of the University of California, Berkeley, I found myself first gravitating toward non-European art and then committing myself to an art history master's degree program at San Francisco State University (SFSU). I found that the arts of Africa exerted the strongest pull. Fortunately, my adviser at SFSU, Professor Judith Bettelheim, was a published specialist in Afro-Caribbean art with a general background that included African art. She had completed doctoral work with Professor Robert Farris Thompson of Yale University, a renowned specialist in both the art of the Yoruba people of southwestern Nigeria and the newly emerging field of African diasporic art. By the late 1990s, the art of Yorubaland had already received sizable scholarly attention in research, publications, and exhibitions. Since my own quite positive exposure, I hoped to find an interesting Yoruba topic that could be handled within the normal master's program time constraints.

Scanning books on contemporary Nigerian art, I came across mention of a Liverpool-born missionary of Irish descent, Rev. Kevin Carroll, of the Society of African Missions (SMA), and the experimental Oye-Ekiti Workshop, active in the period just before Nigeria gained its independence in 1960. Locating this topic's major source, Carroll's 1967 book *Yoruba Religious Carving*,[1] I gleaned enough information to "set the hook" securely. Here was a mid-twentieth-century (1947–54) collaborative art project that involved Catholic priests and Yoruba artists and was designed to do two unusual things: create an indigenous Yoruba-Christian art form for local Christians and promote the local art forms of the region, which were then undergoing rapid change during the last stage of British colonialism. But beyond this key book, virtually nothing significant had been written on the topic.

This bleak research outlook vanished in 2001. The joyful news of the opening of a well-organized archive of the Irish SMA containing Carroll's voluminous records, both written and photographic, changed my prospects and also transformed a basic thesis topic, requiring two weeks of archival work, into an extensive, ongoing project with ever-widening horizons for exploration. This major self-directed Yoruba-Christian project, involving field research in Nigeria and searches through art collections in Nigeria, Italy, New Jersey, and Northern Ireland, finally became the subject of multiple conference papers, journal articles, a planned art exhibition (2012–15), and now this book.

The need for and usefulness of such a work are reinforced by the views of prominent professionals, such as Professor John Picton of the University of London's School of Oriental and African Studies (SOAS), Europe's preeminent center of African studies, who writes, "Father Carroll should be recognized as not simply someone who worked with the 'traditional' . . . artists but as someone who had the vision to look at all aspects of Nigerian art and to work with and otherwise sponsor any artist who was ready to cooperate with the process of transforming the material culture of Catholic Christianity so that it represented the best of contemporary visual culture."[2] A friend and colleague of Father Carroll's since the 1960s, Picton provided generous guidance to this research project and insight for this book.

Two decades ago, William Ostling expressed the currency and timeliness of this book's topic in *Time* magazine in these dramatic words: "Africa is a continent crucified by famine and war, pestilence and poverty.... For Christianity, however, it is a continent of resurrection ... [its] spiritual strength is inspiring—and being inspired by—an outpouring of artistic creation.... Not since Europe's Renaissance has such a large and varied body of living Christian art been produced."[3]

With so little in print regarding African Christian art, I am pleased to be able to offer this account of a recent, intriguing art form of great importance to many readers in this new and changing millennium. At a minimum, I hope that the book's description of the current, difficult conditions under which this genre continues a tenuous existence in many places may contribute to decisions by the mostly ecclesiastical managers to appropriately acknowledge, conserve, and protect this art form and educate the public about its legacy for the future.

ACKNOWLEDGMENTS

Recognizing the assistance of many people in a decade-long project best begins at the beginning, with various academic personnel. My venture into the fresh field of African art history began with Professor Marilyn Wyman at San Jose State University, who pointed me toward a master's program at San Francisco State University, which offered a concentration in Africa and its diaspora. My adviser in graduate studies at SFSU, Professor Judith Bettelheim, reflected professional training of the best sort, including two of the founders of the young field of African art, Arnold Rubin, a specialist in Nigerian art at the University of California, Los Angeles, and Robert Farris Thompson, the eminent Yale scholar of both the art of the Yoruba people and that of the African-Atlantic world. With her background in African art and specialization in the diasporic arts of the Caribbean, Professor Bettelheim encouraged me to pursue the neglected work of Kevin Carroll. She demanded careful research and professional writing, always balanced with the high expectations she held for her own scholarly work. Her continued support for my project never faltered, even as the work evolved over a decade into its present book form.

West African textile specialist Duncan Clarke, a former doctoral student of John Picton's at SOAS, provided the crucial tip-off on the newly opened SMA archive in Cork. Professor Picton himself was the source of multiple, insightful research suggestions, a learned commentator on the finished manuscript, and generous contributor of the book's foreword and some personal photos. He provided the unique combined perspective of a leading expert in this area of African art history and a friend and associate of Kevin Carroll's from 1961 through the next three decades. My research in collections and libraries in Vatican City and Rome was ably assisted by Curator Ester Console of the Vatican Museum of Ethnology-Missiology. Highly rewarding were the curiosity and assistance of the Urbaniana Library's senior librarian, Antonio Alesiani, whose alert mind led us to the discovery and identification of Father Carroll's Three Kings, from the workshop's 1949 Nativity set long lost in plain sight in a university parlor since 1960. Also helpful with advice and commentary on the manuscript at various points were Professors Catie Cadge-Moore of De Anza College and Cecile Fromont of the University of Chicago.

Father Carroll's missionary society, the Society of African Missions, has assisted extensively and generously in various settings in Africa, Europe, and the United States. Most individual members will remain unnamed, but a few need to be acknowledged. Central to the project was archivist Father Edmund Hogan, Ph.D., of the Irish Province, who set up the Kevin Carroll Collection in Cork in its present form. Father Hogan regularly supplied the records and photographic resources needed for this project from 2002 to the present and tirelessly reviewed and commented on the final manuscript. Special thanks to Father Fachtna O'Driscoll, for his strong belief in the book project, and the Irish Provincial Council for its invaluable support in the book's publication. In the Dromantine Conference Centre, Fathers Des Corrigan and P. J. Gormley assisted me in working with Carroll's many Yoruba art pieces stored there. In Nigeria, the various SMA fathers at St. Leo's and the SMA House of Formation in Bodija in Ibadan, helped me find the *in situ* pieces of Yoruba-Christian art. Very helpful at the society's Casa Generaliza in Rome at different times were Fathers Kavanagh, Mandirola, and Wright. Members of the U.S. Province, and especially their museum director, Robert Koenig, supplied advice, appendix material, and images from their important Yoruba-Christian holdings. The SMA has also proved crucial in the planning for an art exhibition that will complement this book.

The most significant, on-site assistance for this book came from the late and sorely missed Oye-Ekiti Workshop carver Lamidi Olonade Fakeye, one of the last workshop participants. In his eighties at the time, he drove my research assistant and me around northwestern Yorubaland and, most meaningfully of all, to Oye-Ekiti, where he summoned the still-living veterans of the workshop for a brief reunion in the summer of 2006. His invaluable contributions to this project (recollections, insights, personal connections, and his art) and to me personally cannot be overstated. Logistics, long-distance driving, and translating for both my visits to the field in Nigeria were ably handled by Niyi (Emmanuel) Odekanyin, then a bright young graduate student at the University of Ibadan and a friend of Duncan Clarke's, who facilitated my initial contact with Lamidi for this project and generally shared his own cultural and social knowledge, so essential for work and research from Oyo to Ife, Benin City, and Lagos. Today he is a cultural officer in the Ministry of Culture and Tourism in the federal capital, Abuja.

The book's publication itself reflects the astute teamwork of various professional sources: Hal Hershey, Dave Peattie and the BookMatters staff, cover designer Stephanie Malinowski, copy editor Laura Iwasaki, wand artist Shelli Joie, Portuguese translator Melina Mattos, and mapmaker Patrick Cadge-Moore.

Oye-Ekiti: Crossroads of History, Art, and Religion

In the 1940s, Irish missionaries and Yoruba artists in southwestern Nigeria began a unique seven-year experiment in religious art collaboration. In this post–World War II era of the globalization of Christianity and its visuality, this new art form represented a significant creative shift away from both the Catholic Church's usual missionary art practices and the customary art of Yorubaland (see fig. 1 and Sidebar 1, "Vernacular Expression"). Once dismissed simply as a by-product of European colonialism in an African setting, the indigenized Christian art of the Oye-Ekiti Workshop (1947–54) instead marked a dramatic change by challenging the dominant negative colonial attitudes toward local ways of life and by developing cultural pluralism within the still strongly Eurocentric Roman Catholic Church. My original archival research in this area a decade ago revealed the surprising situation of a Catholic mentality divided within itself over the issue of an indigenized Christian art, forward-looking ideas about the local culture contrasting with narrow-mindedness on the part of many Irish missionaries and their Nigerian parishioners.[1] In the years between World War II and Nigeria's independence (1960), this new Yoruba-Christian fusion promoted an appreciation of traditional Yoruba art practices while producing a unique African Christian hybrid art that represents a new model of religious and cultural expression in contemporary African art.

A New Model in African Art

When the Vatican invited missionary managers to send examples of the workshop's art to Rome for the international "Exhibition of Sacred Art

Fig. 1. Palace double-door panels, by Areogun of Osi (1880–1954), Opin-Ekiti carver. The armed, mounted horseman in the lower register is probably a Hausa invader from the wars of the nineteenth century, which left a large impact on northern Yorubaland. Areogun was one of the greatest of the premodern carvers of the Opin villages. Father Carroll eventually recruited him to carve for the Oye-Ekiti Workshop in 1952. (By permission of Fowler Museum, UCLA)

Fig. 2. This second exhibition Nativity set from 1951 was made by the Oye-Ekiti Workshop for the Vatican's Archbishop Celso Costantini after the "Exhibition of Sacred Art from the Missionlands," in Rome, 1950. (By permission of Pro Civitate Christiana, Assisi, Italy)

from the Missionlands" in 1950, they selected special works by local artists in the small town of Oye, in the rural Ekiti district of Nigeria (see map, p. 4). Prominent among the artworks from this era are two Christmas Nativity sets, a popular Christian devotional grouping that includes the Holy Family and the Three Kings, or Wise Men or Magi (see fig. 2). These exhibition Nativity sets reflect Yoruba artistic practices of the Ekiti region merged with European Christian ideas and were intended for use in Catholic churches in Nigeria. Crafted between 1949 and 1951 and shipped separately to Italy for the Rome exhibition, the Nativity sets certainly involved a very considerable investment of time and creative energy and were carefully conceived by the artists and their missionary patrons. Incorporating a mixed-media art program of wood carving, beadwork, embroidery, leatherwork, and textile work, these sets exemplify a radical experiment in adapting Yoruba art forms to the expression of Christian ideas for a West African audience and simultaneously contextualizing European Christianity within the way of life of the people of Yorubaland. At the same time, these Rome exhibition pieces

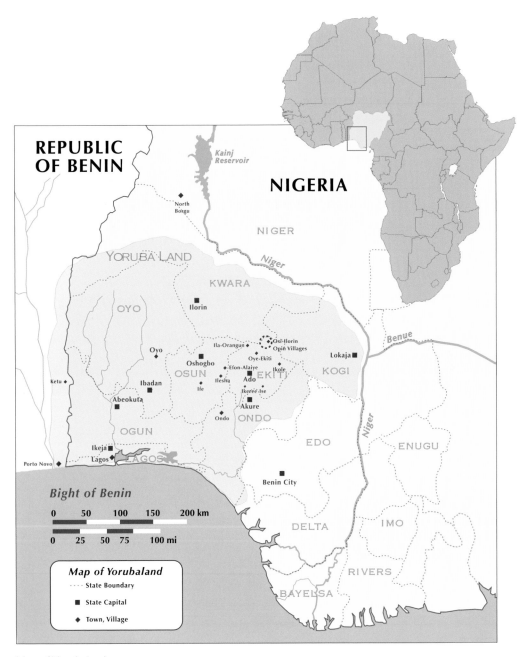

Map of Yorubaland

represent the collaborative desire of the artists to fuse the missionaries' innovative expectations with their own style of artistry in gratifying ways.

Viewed from today's perspective, these Nativity sets from the workshop's early years present snapshots taken midway in the process of indigenizing Christian art in a major African culture. Father Kevin Francis Carroll (1920–1993), the workshop's de facto arts manager, and his artists had moved toward their goal but seemed to hesitate just short of a huge visual leap. In both clothing and features, the Three Kings appear as traditional Yoruba *oba* (kings). The Holy Family's physical features also seem quite compatible with an African identity except when seen alongside those of the darker-skinned Kings (see ch. 4). The workshop envisioned this new hybrid art form as a replacement for the highly Romanticized nineteenth-century European Christian visual expression that European missionaries brought from home and disseminated widely, usually the only imagery to which they had access. In European colonial settings, a blond, blue-eyed Christ could easily be (mis)interpreted as a partner in the imperial power system (see Sidebar 1, "Vernacular Expression").

Mixed Reception

Ranging from appreciation and praise to neglect, rejection, and even vandalism, the public, clerical, and scholarly reactions to this innovative Africanized Christian art have been highly mixed in the sixty years since its introduction. Although a cultural backlash and other complaints from elements within the Catholic community doomed the workshop's brief experimental life, Kevin Carroll continued his collaboration with artists from the Yoruba and other ethnicities in Nigeria's southwest and Middle Belt from 1954 until his death in 1993. While the prolific art traditions of the Yoruba people from southwestern Nigeria belong to one of the longest continuous historical records of any African culture and have been much written about since the 1970s, in-depth coverage of this important Yoruba art innovation has been largely missing from the scholarly and ecclesiastical record for the past half century.

Featuring experimental ideas within the framework of Yoruba carving styles and encountering opposition and criticism due to their radical shift in both viewer perspective and representation at the time, these Nativity sets present major Christian ideas in the process of becoming African ideas against a backdrop of colonial and religious Eurocentrism and racism. This biography of a unique and historic art genre addresses the questions of how

SIDEBAR 1. VERNACULAR EXPRESSION

In the last half of the nineteenth century, Christian missionaries, who preceded, accompanied, or followed European merchants and military and government officials into sub-Saharan Africa, brought with them aspects of their Western European cultures, most notably their visual culture. Religious imagery was often an important instrument in the missionary tool chest. For the most part, Protestant missionaries of Calvinist background eschewed religious imagery, whereas Catholics and Anglicans typically relied heavily on sacred pictures and images as part of their educational approach and in the furnishings of sacred spaces.

The imagery often employed by Catholics had been current in nineteenth-century Europe, especially in France and Italy (see SB fig.1). As is evident in this late-nineteenth-century French Nativity holy card, French neo-Romantic imagery was heavily devotional and descended from the Catholic Reformation and Baroque styles. This kind of devotional art stresses feeling, internal observation, idealized spiritual states, nontheological views, and strong emotions as opposed to representational strategies, such as realism or naturalism. A Nativity scene might easily include a blond, blue-eyed, red-lipped Christ Child, features that could well appear sentimental and unrealistic to modern-day viewers. The Holy Family figures usually have a clearly European appearance. When shepherds are included, their features are sometimes also European, although they might wear a kaffiyeh. The Three Kings of Matthew's Gospel, in which they are identified as coming from "the east," were frequently portrayed more exotically, in Ottoman or other dress then associated with Turkey and the eastern Mediterranean.

Offrons au petit enfant dans la crèche nos cœurs, à lui, qui nous a donné le sien.

SB fig. 1. French Nativity holy card, 1898. The card illustrates the type of Christian art Archbishop Celso Costantini, the Vatican's secretary of Propaganda Fide, would criticize beginning in the 1930s as "foreign in feeling" when used in non-European mission contexts. (Collection of the author)

and why those central Christian ideas would become African art both in the relationship of the artists and their missionary patrons at Oye-Ekiti and in that art's continuing, though sometimes contested, reception. And, finally, the epilogue to this account completes the narrative of Yoruba-Christian art up to the present by summarizing my search for the legacy of this significant genre today.

Overlooked by Scholars

While usually acknowledging that the Oye-Ekiti Workshop developed a unique art form, Africanist art historians often move on to other, presumably more interesting, developments in Nigeria in the same period, perhaps because the workshop is not yet perceived by some as "breaking loose from the shackles of colonial thinking."[2] Marginal treatment of Yoruba-Christian art misses its deeper significance in Nigerian contemporary artistic and cultural history. Art historian John Clark observes that "while the modern [in art] appears as a break [with the past], its radicality is more in the relativization of forms than in the absolute rendering of forms redundant in terms of some narrative of progress or development."[3] His point is apt, although he focuses on a break with the past in form, whereas Carroll and the workshop's artists changed the narrative content rather than the form of Yoruba visual expression.

Also missed by many observers are the even greater historic shifts represented by the explosive southward expansion of Christianity in Africa, Asia, and Latin America and the rapid globalization of Christianity during the past half century. So dramatic and opposite from the familiar broad historical patterns dating back to the nineteenth and earlier centuries of European expansion, these changes might collectively be termed a "Great Reversal." In Africa alone, the number of Christians increased from about ten million in 1900 to almost four hundred million by 2004.[4] Another source puts the number of Christians in the world today at 2.1 billion and the total membership of the Catholic Church itself at 1.1 billion, despite sizable losses in Europe.[5] In the religion's third millennium, some Christians emigrating from the Southern Hemisphere are heading for Europe and North America as missionaries, to proselytize among their secular diasporic populations. For Africans, Christianity certainly continues to be an agent of globalization, as scholars are beginning to recognize.[6] On the global scale, these changes presage the conversion of Christianity into a predominantly non-Western, nonwhite, culturally diverse global religion in the twenty-first century. The Oye-Ekiti Workshop heralded these momentous, demographic shifts.

Embodying ten years of research conducted across three continents, this illustrated and narrative work reflects recent multidisciplinary analysis of published and unpublished archival and museum resources as well as field-work in Ireland, Italy, Nigeria, Vatican City, and the United States. It sheds new light on the crucial roles of three Church figures. The first is missionary art theorist the Reverend Dr. Patrick J. Kelly (1904–1988), who conceived, established, and staffed the workshop in Oye-Ekiti. The second was a crucial source of Kelly's motivation, the high-ranking and visionary Vatican leader Cardinal Celso Costantini (1877–1958), whose theory of adaptation (later called "inculturation"), expounded in Rome in the 1930s, exerted much critical influence on the workshop (see ch. 1).[7] And the third figure, from a more remote time, is the founder of Carroll's African-focused missionary society, Bishop Melchior de Marion Brésillac (1800–1856) of France, who emphasized that the ultimate purpose of his foundation was the creation of an indigenous Catholic clergy, rather than "conversions." This book also traces the development of the Yoruba-Christian art experiment as it evolved through initial theoretical stages into a distinct genre of African art (see ch. 5).

Christianity and Art in Africa

While the spread of Christianity is a major theme of modern African his-tory and of world historical significance, the relationship of Christianity to African art is "the great unresearched topic," according to John Picton.[8] The 1989 cover story by William Ostling, *Time* magazine's veteran religion edi-tor, appropriately credited the Oye-Ekiti Workshop as a starting point for a parallel "latter-day art boom" in African Christian art.[9] And, according to J. D. Y. Peel, an anthropologist at the University of London, the "large-scale adoption of Christianity has been one of the master themes of modern African history" and "may well prove to be of world historical significance, too, contributing to the decisive shift in Christianity's geopolitical placement from North to South."[10] Surprisingly, the art historical coverage of Africa's Christian art in the explosive twentieth century is little studied or writ-ten about, and the subject has been skimmed over or ignored in recent and acclaimed African art history texts.

Only partially aware of developments outside the conventional areas of current African art scholarship—that is, ethnographic and international or contemporary practice—even prominent sources on art practices since the mid-twentieth century provide but a bare mention of Africa's Christian art. One would assume that little Christian art is being produced that is worthy of study. Yet, on a continent where the number of Christians surpasses four hundred million and where it is rare to meet someone who does not self-identify with a religion, it is hard to believe that there is so little African Christian art for African art historians to research and comment on (see Sidebar 2, "Revising the Missionary Stereotype").

A Biography of an Art Form

This book, then, represents a biography of a small, but important genre of mid-twentieth-century African art, an early step in recognizing the artistic significance and global significance of the visual expression of African Christianity. This biography includes closely related projects—first, the main account of the Oye-Ekiti arts workshop and its Yoruba-Christian fusion and, second, a brief summary of the decade-long search for this genre's legacy and acceptance that followed. *Africanizing Christian Art* provides a case study of the earliest institutional missionary attempt at adapting Christianity to an indigenous African cultural context and the subsequent fate of these artworks in the hands of Western institutions.

Since these missionary-artists, whose lives had been dedicated to the creation and success of this indigenous Christian art form, had died by the time my project began, and the available print sources eventually ran dry, a limited narrative would have left the fate of the Yoruba-Christian genre, the heritage of Kevin Carroll and his Nigerian collaborators, incomplete, lacking even a recent snapshot, much less a reasonably accurate contemporary portrait. Consequently, as researcher, author, and ultimately passionate devotee of the genre, I faced the question of its legacy: What did the missionary art patrons and their collaborating artists hand down to the present? And what has survived for us in the field and in various Western institutions, and under what individual conditions?

This Yoruba-Christian art form presents enduring relevance as an interesting artistic model, continues to be useful as an expressive option in contemporary church settings, and is an instructive and illuminating case study in Christian indigenization. The epilogue describes the continuing mixed reception of Yoruba-Christian art by those for whom it was designed, by

SIDEBAR 2. REVISING THE MISSIONARY STEREOTYPE

The unique SMA program fostering the creation of Yoruba-Christian hybrid art seems a radical role reversal for Christian missionaries, who are often stereotyped as agents of imperialism and implacable enemies of local religious practice and cultural expression. While conventional missionary attitudes and practices inevitably rejected indigenous African art as the vehicle of "paganism," anthropologist J. D. Y. Peel, of the University of London's School of Oriental and African Studies, has presented a more nuanced and accurate view, highlighting the crucial role of Christian missionaries in the process of Yoruba "ethnogenesis," in formulating a standard Yoruba culture (language, traditional religion, and ethnic identity) integral to the process of Christianizing the region. Relying on archives of the Anglican Church Missionary Society (CMS) and the historical experiences of the first generation of missionaries in what became southwestern Nigeria, Peel has recently provided an extensive revision of this missionary stereotype.[1] He convincingly shows that, through their encounter with these missions, the Yoruba came to know themselves as a distinct people beginning in the mid-nineteenth century. And in this process, Yoruba culture, especially its language and music, became a vehicle for the conversion of Anglican Christianity into a local religion. The first wave of CMS missionaries into Yorubaland included Yoruba-speaking converts recruited in Sierra Leone from among the Yoruba people who had been freed and resettled there after the interruption of slave trading by the British navy's intervention. Through this growing base of Yoruba-speaking teachers, catechists, and clergy, the missionaries developed a standard Yoruba language out of the many dialects and soon enshrined it in a Yoruba-Christian Bible, liturgy, and music.[2] In Peel's words, "the Christian clergy were ethnic missionaries, and, being pan-Yoruba, played key mediating roles in resolving conflicts between warring states by the 1880s."[3] These Protestant missionaries constituted a new cultural agency, promoting an explicit process of regional cultural integration along with the Gospel and constructing a Christian Yoruba intelligentsia and the base of modern Yoruba nationalism.[4]

---

1. Peel 1989, Peel 2001.

2. Picton 2002, 100.

3. Peel 1989, 201.

4. Peel 1989, 198.

those for whom it was intended as an instrument of evangelization, and by those who preserve such expressive, visual activities and objects. Since artwork can long endure under varying conditions, a critical narrative of this art (a scholarly biography of an art form, if you will) should not cease, even if the original circumstances and people associated with its creation are past; consequently, though briefly, this account follows the genre from its roots up to the present.

A decade of fieldwork beyond the archive included visits to sites on three continents (Africa, Europe, and North America), encounters with dozens of people and institutions with various connections to the art, and many surprises. Ultimately, the fieldwork became a personal quest to discover the current fate of Oye-Ekiti's art itself. This hunt for Father Carroll's legacy, briefly described in the epilogue, reflects the current scattered character of the workshop's progeny and the sometimes insecure conditions of its existence. This legacy question unavoidably poses the further issue of the role of Church-related institutions, from local parish churches and cathedrals in Nigeria to prestigious Vatican museums and a university, in preserving the cultural and religious heritage of non-European peoples entrusted to their care. This volume offers no more than a sketch of the wide variety of circumstances that Yoruba-Christian art continues to experience, from professional curatorial care to outright neglect, vandalism, and loss.

Globalizing and Localizing Christianity

"There is nothing distinctive about the earliest Christian art except its subject matter," comments Andrew Walls, Scottish missiologist and professor of religious studies. "It brought no style, form, or technique that was not already employed in pagan Roman art.... Christian art needs vernacular expression, a sense of locality ... the Word became flesh and spoke Aramaic; presumably with a Galilean accent."[1] With this wry Gospel paraphrase, Walls suggests that, by its nature, Christianity does not necessarily belong to a single people, place, language, race, or culture and instead has always relied on expansion that has involved "the serial, generational, and vernacular penetration of different cultures."[2] As a world religion, which emerged from a west Asian Jewish context and moved to many other contexts, including, prominently, a European one, Christianity has transmitted and adapted beliefs and practices across different linguistic and cultural boundaries for two millennia.

A Global Context

Previously in its theology, perhaps as far back as the Early Church Fathers, the Catholic Church often held narrow views of non-Christian religions, which it expressed in its most negative, premodern version at the Council of Florence in 1442: "There is no salvation outside the Church."[3] But beginning in this early modern period, often with the Portuguese in Africa and Asia, the Church faced powerful non-European states that outclassed it in resources and strength, and the modern missionary experience emerged, in which the missionary must "live on terms set by others."[4] Consequently, this extreme Florentine axiom was frequently tempered, ignored, or reinterpreted in periods and situations of openness, engagement, and advantage, although the fear of syncretism, creating hybrids of different religions, remained a latent fear in all Christian missionary activity. And during the era of European exploration and expansion (1400–1800), the Roman Catholic Church became not only the first religious body but also the first institution of any kind to operate on a global scale (see Sidebar 3, "Christian Art and Cultural Pluralism"). A Portuguese-led mission to the Kongo kingdom in central Africa, begun in 1491, was an early and successful experience of a Catholic mission to a sub-Saharan African people. Soon after, Christianity became incorporated as part of the indigenous Kongo religion, and the Church went so far as to accept the idea that the local Kongo people had enjoyed the benefits of divine revelations and miracles before the arrival of the Christian emissaries. With this surprisingly open approach, an indigenous clergy and religious art developed from the beginning.[5]

The Catholic Church's cultural adaptation in its contacts with religions other than Judaism and Islam during this era seems heavily influenced by power considerations.[6] In Spanish colonial Mexico, where the Church held extensive political power, its attitude was usually exclusivist. Nevertheless, some limited hybridization was sometimes tolerated, especially at the margins of Spanish control. Yet in Ming dynasty China, a location where the Church and its missionaries had no political power, extensive accommodation of Confucianism in rites and art took place during the Jesuit mission of Matteo Ricci (1583–1610).[7] In order to manage its global missionary efforts, the papacy created a ministry of missionary efforts in 1622, the Sacred Congregation of the Propagation of the Faith, better known by its abbreviated Latin name, Propaganda Fide. This agency initially combined and oversaw the activities of the Church's growing missionary efforts outside of Europe following the Catholic Reformation.

Coincident with the nineteenth-century colonial expansion of the rapidly industrializing western European nations, but stemming from additional roots, a revival of earlier European missionary efforts and organizations in both Catholic and Protestant religious communities appeared throughout western Europe, especially in France. Buoyed by a swell of Romanticism in popular literature and arts (which often included idealized accounts of missionary exploits), as well as an interest in exploration, trade,

SIDEBAR 3. CHRISTIAN ART AND CULTURAL PLURALISM

Not surprisingly, European Christian missionaries generally employed their own familiar art styles and conventions in their visual communication with non-Europeans. Some notable exceptions did occur, however, when indigenous imagery as well as local religious ideas were integrated with conventional European Catholic art.

An early and successful Catholic mission to a sub-Saharan African people began in 1491 as a Portuguese-led mission to the Kongo kingdom in Central Africa. Soon after, Christianity was incorporated as part of the indigenous Kongo religion and the Church went so far as to accept that the local Bakongo people had benefited from divine revelations and miracles before the arrival of the Christian emissaries. With this favorable interpretation, an indigenous clergy and religious art developed from the beginning, without the imposition of biblical images in Western form.[1] Vestiges of this art have survived in the syncretistic use of crucifixes and statues of the Virgin and saints (see SB fig. 2).[2]

In colonial Mexico, the Church held extensive political power, and its attitude was usually exclusivist; at times, the Spanish Inquisition and other forms of violence were employed.

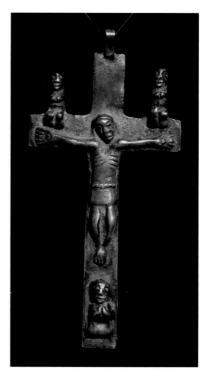

SB fig. 2. Brass pectoral crucifix of the Kongo peoples in central Africa, seventeenth century. Evidence of Christianity's early modern era acceptance and indigenous Christian art production in central Africa, the cross is a recent donation to the collection of the African Art Museum of the SMA Fathers, Tenafly, N.J. (SMA-USA)

and colonial expansion, missionary activity "again became fashionable in Catholic circles."[8] The competitiveness of rival colonial powers could hardly have exceeded the competitiveness of Catholic and Protestant missionaries. And where colonial administrators took control, they were always preceded by, accompanied by, or closely followed by missionaries.[9] This missionary impulse did not much affect Irish Catholics during most of the nineteenth

SB fig. 3. Altar canopy, Church of San Jose, Laguna Pueblo, New Mexico, shows the inclusion of indigenous Sun and Moon images associated closely with a depiction of the Holy Trinity under Spanish Franciscans before the Anglo-American period of the nineteenth century. (NJB)

Nevertheless, it sometimes tolerated limited hybridization, especially at the margins of political control. At the farthest northern end of direct ecclesiastical control and influence were the Franciscan missionary establishments in the upper Rio Grande Valley, located in what is now New Mexico, in the indigenous Pueblo communities. After the 1680 Pueblo Revolt, returning Franciscan missionaries sometimes recognized that a softer, inclusive approach to the indigenous culture might be appropriate. This early nineteenth-century Pueblo altar canopy painting, which combines prominent indigenous Sun and Moon imagery with a portrayal of the Holy Trinity, is one example of this limited fusion (see SB fig. 3). In Ming dynasty China, where the Church had no political power, Catholic rites and art accommodated Confucianism at the imperial court during the Jesuit mission of Matteo Ricci.[3]

(continued)

century, but by the early part of the twentieth century, cultural and political forces were stirring that favored a national missionary movement, much of which was focused in the Anglophone colonial areas under British control.

Nevertheless, the Great Missionary Movement (as the widespread European Christian expansionism of the late nineteenth and early twentieth centuries is known) initially carried with it a great deal of ethnocentric cultural

SIDEBAR 3 *(continued)*

In order to manage, coordinate, and promote its global missionary efforts, the papacy under Pope Urban VIII created a ministry of missionary supervision in 1622, the Sacred Congregation of the Propagation of the Faith, or Propaganda Fide.] Formed during the Catholic Reformation, this bureaucracy initially combined and oversaw activities intended to regain territory and peoples recently lost to Protestantism but soon refocused its attention on the Church's growing extra-European missionary efforts. Five years later, Urban established a college to further the Vatican's missionary aims, namely, the Pontifical Urbaniana University (see SB figs. 4 and 5).

SB fig. 4. Since 1623, the Palazzo di Propaganda Fide has housed the Catholic Church's ministry of missions, now called the Congregation of the Evangelization of the Peoples, at this location on Rome's Piazza di Spagna. (NJB)

---

1. Thornton 1984, 149.

2. Shorter 1996, 63.

3. Bailey 1999, 95–105.

SB fig. 5. The Pontifical Urbaniana University in Vatican City, founded in 1627, specializes in training missionaries for the Church outside of Europe. (NJB)

baggage, nearly as much as the colonialist movement of the same period with which it was long, but inaccurately, identified. The Eurocentrism, or dominance of European attitudes, within the nineteenth- and early-twentieth-century African mission systems of both Protestant and Catholic churches reflects their common strategy of training a Christian, European-shaped elite. And, "on the whole, with some important exceptions, the European missionaries knew little of the culture, traditional values, and religious beliefs of the people, but rather strictly condemned everything in their way of life and religion," according to missiologist Jon Kirby.[10] These attitudes prevailed not only among the mission clergy but among scholars, officials, and much of the European intelligentsia. In a modern sense, missionaries in Africa, and indeed most of the personnel associated with both the colonial and mission projects, did not recognize their targeted populations as complete cultures. In general, and especially before World War II, nearly all mission-related churches required their neophytes to renounce almost all contact with their traditional systems of worship and related practices, including their art. As Kirby also writes, "Proper European civilization was Christianity, and the only way to bring about conversion was to establish this (European) cultural framework. . . . Indeed anything else was unthinkable."[11]

Cultural Awareness

Though usually hostile to non-European religions and cultures, the Roman Catholic Church slowly extended its theological perspectives and began correcting the cultural and aesthetic ethnocentrism and iconoclasm of its earlier missionaries by the end of the nineteenth century. As early as 1870, when missionaries were encountering vast numbers of non-Europeans, the harsh theoretical formulas of earlier centuries began to soften.[12] By the early twentieth century, this slow change in thinking became noticeable. The Vatican began to make distinctions between an indigenous religion and the rest of the culture (especially art) among non-European peoples, although few anthropological studies of African religion or art were available to challenge common misconceptions.

Beginning in 1903, a series of papal encyclicals observed that the Church now left final decisions on sacred art to local bishops, a recognition that good (including "good" art, presumably) could be found in every part of the world.[13] By the 1920s, the upper levels of the Church had developed some cross-cultural sensitivities and came belatedly to an appreciation of non-

European art, including the art of Africa, under the sympathetic pontificate of Pius XI (1922–39), sometimes called the Missionary Pope. At the same time, a second and more important key indicator of progress in cultural pluralism and decolonization occurred when Pius's encyclical in 1926 banned discrimination against non-European clergy ("Let there be no discrimination or caste distinction between European and local clergy," *Rerum Eclesiae*) on the occasion of the consecration of the first six local Chinese Catholic bishops, an essential step in the establishment of an indigenous Catholic Church in what had once been called simply "missionland." Slowly, the Vatican moved to decolonize its structure in non-European regions. Though not directly related, these changes in the Vatican's perceptions of non-European peoples paralleled the recognition, acceptance, and development of the study of African and other non-Western art and culture by Euro-American artists and the secular academy.

Celso Costantini

A prime mover in this fresh interest in and insight into the cultures and art of the "missionlands" was Archbishop Celso Costantini (1877–1958), who served as the apostolic delegate (papal representative) in China from 1922 to 1935 during the development of a native Chinese hierarchy in the 1920s. He also witnessed the impact of Japanese military aggression in Manchuria in the early 1930s. This perceptive prelate, who served as the secretary, or manager, of the Vatican's ministry for the missions, Propaganda Fide, from 1935 to 1953 (see fig. 3), began shaping an evolving concept initially called *adaptation* but subsequently termed the *theology of inculturation* in Catholic usage following the Second Vatican Council (1962–65) or indigenization or contextualization elsewhere.

As developed and published by Costantini in 1940, the theory of inculturation proposed that the Church should encourage Christianity to flourish within the local culture (and, notably, its artistic expression) rather than imposing European culture while spreading the Gospel.[14] Based on his observations and experiences of the brutal imposition of Japanese imperial rule in war-torn China, Costantini observed: "Because the missions were organized by a foreign hierarchy with the help of foreign governments marked by a foreign imperialistic spirit, it is no wonder that the [Christian] art was also foreign"[15] (see SB fig. 1). The author of scholarly works on Christian art his-

Fig. 3. Celso Costantini, papal ambassador to China, became Secretary of Propaganda Fide (1935–53) and an early advocate of inculturation, or indigenization, of Christian imagery for non-European cultures. (By permission of Archivio Storico, Evangelization of Peoples, Vatican City)

tory and the training of indigenous clergy, Costantini specifically focused on non-European Christian art in this introduction to cultural adaptation that constituted the most extensive survey to date in that field. "Foreign feeling and Europeanism must stop at the threshold of our churches," he forcefully concluded as his recommendation for missions in the future.[16]

Formulation and encouragement of the inculturation policy by the Church's leadership represented early theoretical steps in the decolonization process of the institutional Catholic Church in Africa, through the development of cultural pluralism along with an indigenous clergy and hierarchy. Hoping to stimulate the development of local Christian arts in Asia and Africa, Costantini had successfully lobbied Pope Pius XI by 1937 to promote inculturation in the arts by calling for the Vatican's international "Exhibition of the Art of the Missionlands," scheduled initially for 1940. Although it was postponed because of the pope's death and the outbreak of World War II, his successor, Pius XII (1939–1958), also backed the idea of an exhibition, which was eventually held in Rome during the Holy Year celebrations in 1950.[17]

As a response to this encouragement and challenge from the highest level of the Catholic Church, the Oye-Ekiti art workshop in colonial Nigeria represents a significant development in this early stage of Africanizing Christianity in the twentieth century. From another perspective, it is a way of helping a person figure out how to be both a Christian and an African at the same time without having to become European in the process.

Dr. Kelly's Scheme:
An Artist-Missionary

An energetic, bright, and insightful seminarian in his early thirties, immersed in doctoral studies in Rome between 1932 and 1938, Patrick Martin Kelly became acquainted with the currents of thought and discourse circulating in the higher echelons of the Catholic Church (see fig. 4). As a member of the Society of African Missions, Kelly became especially focused on any new thinking within Vatican circles as it applied to missionary work. What he heard would change his life as a member of the Society's Irish Province, which staffed schools and churches in Anglophone Nigeria and other British colonial territories in West Africa.

New Ideas in Rome

During the late 1930s, the gifted, art-oriented, visionary thinker and prelate Archbishop Celso Costantini, serving as secretary of Propaganda Fide, captured Kelly's attention. In China, following the Japanese seizure of Manchuria, Costantini had witnessed the devastating effects of foreign imperialism on the people and government of this huge but hapless nation, the target of aggressive colonial powers for much of the previous century. He realized something that seems commonsensical today, that because foreign missionaries were outsiders, often from the colonizing nations, their religious message could not avoid including much cultural baggage.

On the evidence of their eyes and ears, Costantini believed, the local people inevitably understood the Church's message, spread primarily by

Fig. 4. Reverend Dr. Patrick M. "Doc" Kelly, SMA, youthful yet farsighted reformer and Irish provincial (1946–52) who instigated the Oye-Ekiti Scheme for creating an indigenous Christian art for the Church in Nigeria. (Kevin Carroll Collection [KCC], Cork, Ireland)

its European missionaries, as an alien one. Based on his East Asian experience, this dynamic prelate believed that this kind of proselytizing in China required Chinese Christian recruits to become virtual Europeans in the process of Christian conversion. Consequently, he became both a cultural pluralist and a universalist within the Vatican leadership, and a strong voice advocating the adaptation of Christianity to the local culture, By 1940, he had published the most extensive and comprehensive history of Christian art outside of Europe, which vehemently advocated the development of an indigenous Christian art for use in the Church's missions.

Dr. Kelly's Reforms

After some formative years of exposure to these fresh insights, Kelly (sometimes called "Doc" within the Society and, more formally, "Dr. Kelly" within the larger Nigerian community because of his prestigious Roman doctor of divinity degree) embarked on a series of frustrating mission experiences at SMA schools in British Nigeria. With firsthand experience, the Irish reformer came to resent the British colonial system and believed that existing missionary schools trained students too much for "the clerk's stool," mostly producing clerical labor for British bureaucratic and commercial interests, and had little respect for the cultural and social realities of local people (see Sidebar 2, "Revising the Missionary Stereotype"). Frequently transferred from one posting to another before he could implement any reforms, Kelly developed his vision, which led to a strongly self-sufficient, vocationally oriented Christian community adapted to the local way of life. As later embodied in the Oye-Ekiti Workshop, Kelly's ideas seem to blend some of his society's nineteenth-century idealistic, communitarian, and experimental values with the refreshing new theology of Archbishop (later Cardinal) Costantini's cultural adaptation.[1] Supported by his order's tradition of respect for the local culture (see Appendix), the Vatican's latest teachings, and his own recent frustration and discontent in the field, Kelly began brewing a radical mixture for the era, for his order's Irish Province, and for the Nigerian mission setting.

Rapidly formulating his highly reformist vision in practical terms and articulating it at the Society's Irish Provincial Assembly in 1946, the passionate Kelly impressed the other delegates, who elected him on a wave of enthusiasm as religious superior of the Irish Province (the provincial) for a renewable six-year term (1946–52). Embracing the approach of African independence following World War II, the charismatic Kelly's highest priority for the province quickly became the realization of his innovative and unconventional goals in education and cultural adaptation. With the province's human and financial resources now at his disposal, Kelly began planning what soon became known in the province as the "Oye-Ekiti Scheme," reflecting the experimental nature of the project.

Kelly proposed starting with an arts workshop, which would serve as a demonstration center or showcase and develop in time into a full-fledged vocational college. He considered its location, situated far from more Europeanized places, like the colonial cities Lagos and Ibadan in Nigeria, and indeed from any big towns and large settlements, a matter of the greatest importance. He believed that in a rural setting, remote from imported influences, "where traditional lore is still dispensed around the fire," people would be more "representative of their country and culture." In this idealized setting, "their arts and crafts can be developed, no longer for mere utility, but also for beauty and inspiration hitherto unsuspected."[2] With such "traditionalizing" views (as opposed to the more typical missionary's modernizing goals), Kelly believed African social problems could be corrected only by Africans, but only when they were educated, "not so much in the book, but in the soul."[3] Hardly a true modernizer, Kelly wanted everything suggestive of a foreign culture, with the exception of Christianity, to be excluded, hoping to "restore Yoruba culture to some kind of mythic Christianized purity."[4]

In Kelly's vision, a new kind of missionary, an "artist who really under-stood African culture," would conceive the center's art and supervise students in its development: "Everything needed for divine liturgy should issue from the artist's mind and the craftsman's hands."[5] His working approach to adap-tation began with the local culture as the basis of all Christianizing efforts. In the previous century, his society's founder, Bishop Melchior de Marion Brésillac, had stressed respect for the host African societies' ways of life in his strong advocacy of the necessity, urgency, and practicality of forming indige-nous clergy. Following Costantini's injunction against the violent imposition of European culture, Kelly encouraged the careful study of the people and their lives, language, customs, religious beliefs, economy, and social system before adapting Christianity's superstructure.[6] Kelly's "artist" was the proto-type of a new indigenizing missionary–art collaborator–patron: the artistic, cultural specialist, fully conversant in the local culture, lifestyle, and social situation. Such an art patron–ethnologist–minister would lead new con-verts gradually from their traditional values "to the higher and purer value of Christian faith and morals."[7] For Kelly, little of what the Europeans built in Africa would survive their departure, unless it were built "on a sure founda-tion—Africa itself and the Africans."[8]

The Workshop Idea

As called for in his imaginative blueprint, the initial development would be a centralized art workshop. This first stage would use a newly Africanized Christian art to showcase how Christian culture could permeate African life as a whole. Despite the prominence given to new art in Kelly's scheme, the Church in West Africa had no models to guide him. And in any case, for Kelly, art should not be imposed or imparted; rather, the inculturating missionary could "only awaken it, elicit it and facilitate its expression," and then, with proper management, the art production "could be used so that a 'cultured' African art will find expression in . . . Religion."[9] In this way, Kelly tried to suggest the appropriate balance that would enable the missionary–art patron to somehow guide African artists without imposing cold "foreign concepts" on them. Certainly, developing practical and theoretical methods for collaboration between missionaries and artists would be one of the most important goals of his scheme. Although Kelly was later criticized within the society for spending too much time on the workshop's inculturation proj-ect and not enough on administrative issues in his tenure as provincial, his ideas nevertheless reflect the influence of the leading edge of contemporary Vatican teachings on cultural pluralism and demonstrate definite continuities with SMA ideals and practices in Nigeria as expressed by the SMA's founder, Bishop Brésillac, who emphasized recruiting an indigenous clergy and cultivating respect for the host cultural group.

Staffing the Workshop

Kelly's earlier attempts at reform and innovation in the mission field taught him that two basic requirements were lacking: talented, sympathetic personnel and a setting conducive to building a new type of institution from the ground up. He knew from previous experience that such a daring venture required at least two, and likely three, dedicated long-term managers. By 1946, he had identified two promising candidates for his scheme, both young and rather new to mission work but lacking the narrow Eurocentric mind-set that he saw among an older generation of missionaries. In addition, both possessed artistic and technical skills and were open to a radically different approach to missionary work.

The new provincial enthusiastically recruited Kevin Francis Carroll, who had been born in Liverpool, United Kingdom, in 1920 to Irish parents. As a child, Carroll had met a family friend who happened to be an SMA missionary on leave from Liberia.[10] After this casual introduction to someone with firsthand experience of missionary life, Carroll, a studious young man with an interest in natural history, art, and ornithology, entered and completed the order's seminary program at Dromantine (County Down) in Northern Ireland, receiving priestly ordination in 1942 (see fig. 5).[11] A modest painter in his own right, Carroll was stationed in 1943 in a Catholic teacher-training college in the Gold Coast colony (Ghana), where he taught arts and crafts to the students and acquainted himself with local wood carving and kente cloth–weaving techniques.[12] While in Ghana, he obtained an English copy of Costantini's 1940 book on adaptation, which had a great influence on him.[13]

Also part of the start-up management team for Kelly's daring workshop program, the athletic Sean Oliver Plunkett "Seano" O'Mahony (1920–2001) likewise shared an interest in and aptitude for art; as a student, he had worked on stage scenery and graphic design. A few years out of secondary school, O'Mahony fulfilled his interest in becoming a missionary by joining the SMA and completing his preparation and ordination in June 1946,

 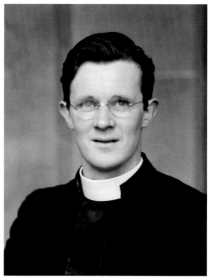

Fig. 5 *(left)*. Reverend Kevin Francis Carroll was born in Liverpool, Great Britain, and entered the Society of African Missions at an early age. He was ordained a priest late in 1942 and, after a few years in the British Gold Coast Colony (Ghana), was recruited for Dr. Kelly's project because of his clear interest in the arts of Africa. (KCC)

Fig. 6 *(right)*. Reverend Sean Oliver Plunkett "Seano" O'Mahony joined the Society of African Missions and, because of his interest in art, was selected for Dr. Kelly's innovative art project in 1946. He spent some months developing his art and building skills in Great Britain before joining Carroll at the small town of Oye-Ekiti by the beginning of 1948. (KCC)

coinciding with Kelly's first year as provincial and the instigation of his arts venture (see fig. 6).

Kelly intended Carroll to fill the first position in developing and managing the arts and O'Mahony to take the clay- and brick-production and construction role, but he never successfully staffed the third and, in retrospect, crucial slot of general manager on a long-term continuous basis. The two young priests probably shared the general management duties to some extent when management drifted, but it seems that the more verbal and assertive Carroll informally assumed more of this role than the hands-on, pragmatic O'Mahony, especially in communicating with the various outside agencies: the diocese, the SMA, the Church, and local and colonial governmental authorities. No third member of the team stayed long enough to provide the much-needed, long-term support and management as well as effective public relations, education, and marketing within the Nigerian Catholic community. This failure to provide crucial staffing in order to promote and explain the workshop and its radical program within the SMA and the broader Nigerian Catholic community (especially the clergy and hierarchy) undoubtedly contributed to the scheme's mixed reception and eventual demise.

The two new missionaries, both twenty-six years old, spent the summer of 1946 in Britain, immersed in an intensive short course in their new field, religious art. They studied Christian liturgical art in the art libraries and museums of London, especially the Victoria and Albert and the British Museum with its large African holdings. They also observed contemporary British liturgical art production, including vestment design and pottery making.[14] O'Mahony studied construction materials and techniques, such as brick making. He and Carroll consulted with Rev. Bede Griffiths, a pioneering English Benedictine monk on his way to India, who specialized in cross-cultural religious dialogue and inculturation. The three missionaries also discussed the project with Maxwell Frye and his wife, Jane Drew, modernist British architects concentrating on tropical architecture. They had worked for the colonial government in Nigeria during World War II and advised the three clerics to develop an organic plan on location after surveying, soil sampling, and vegetation and hydrologic studies were done. The project would develop on site and thus avoid too much advance planning.[15] All of this very generalized preparation clearly helped the neophytes in the work of launching the radically new art experiment, although they were embarking on a voyage into the unknown.

The Workshop and the Artists: Traditional Skills to New Purposes

In developing a new African Christian art form, Kelly envisioned a workshop that would function as the first phase of his larger scheme of building an African-centered vocational, technical college. He and the two young priests considered a number of factors in situating the workshop in Yorubaland in southwestern Nigeria, where the Society of African Missions had an eighty-five-year history of mission activity (see map, p. 4). Kelly had expressed a clear preference for a rural location closer to more traditional life ways, as opposed to the larger colonial cities with their westernizing influences.

Locating the Workshop

The Ekiti region in northeastern Yoruba country enjoyed a reputation for long and honored art traditions and seemed well suited to the recruitment of skilled workers for the venture. Importantly for a Catholic project, Thomas Hughes, the bishop of the local Ondo diocese (also a member of the SMA), favored the scheme as serving the needs of a rural community near the dividing line between the northern border of the West African forests and the grassland-savanna, approximately five hundred miles south of the Sahara desert.

In choosing to locate their experimental inculturation project in this part of southwestern Nigeria, Kelly and his young art managers were, whether consciously or not, immersing the workshop (and themselves) within one of the oldest, continuous, and most prolific traditions of visual expression in

West Africa. Cultural heirs of the eleventh-century city-state of Ile-Ife and the seventeenth-century empire of Oyo, the Yoruba-speaking peoples had developed an elaborate system of visual culture based on their religious traditions, local needs and customs, and their many centers of royal power. In previous centuries, the influence of Yoruba art and culture had been extended via the Atlantic slave trade to areas of European colonial domination (Cuba, Brazil, etc.), creating a Yoruba diaspora within the greater African diaspora. Within the Yoruba expressive culture of the late British colonial era and especially in Ekiti and the surrounding districts, wood carving presented a fully realized tradition of monumental royal architectural elements, religious materials, and statuary of documented antiquity. Nevertheless, like other customary arts, it was struggling for survival under the modernizing influences of colonial circumstances.

The well-developed wood-carving tradition of the Ekiti region has been among the best-documented for the colonial period. For example, Africanist art historian Roslyn Walker, in her monograph on one of the most important Yoruba artists of the twentieth century, Olowe of Ise (d. 1938), cites her subject's position within "the prevailing Ekiti-Yoruba stylistic canon and conventions."[1] And John Picton refers to the "great archetypal masters of Opin," a notable local wood-carving tradition within the Ekiti region (see Sidebar 4, "The Opin-Ekiti Carving Tradition").[2]

The eventual site, three miles from the town of Oye in the Ekiti district, impressed Kelly as a good place to begin the experiment: the sufficiently rural setting located at the intersection of four roads included a good source of tile clay, seemed wholesome and pleasant, and was well situated near seventeen villages. The area's people also struck Carroll as promising: they were open to education and "relatively wealthy and progressive," and both the men and women were still involved in "a great variety of the old crafts."[3] In his unpublished diary, Carroll noted approvingly the stream's potential for developing a reservoir, clay for tile and bricks, fertile soil, and good climate.[4]

Despite the demands of creating workshop facilities from scratch on a very low budget, the missionaries spent much time observing the social and cultural patterns of the local community. Through their contacts with the female weavers, all local residents, Carroll and O'Mahony became aware of the local Yoruba religious calendar of festivals and other ritual observances. These practices, all intimately interwoven with the seasonal weather and agricultural cycles, still held great sway within the whole community, regardless of religious affiliation.[5] Witnessing the still-pervasive influence of Yoruba tradition on not only the non-Christians but also the local mission congregation undoubtedly encouraged the priests in their enterprise of translating the Christian message within the visual expression of local culture. These experiences initiated Carroll into the exploration of Yoruba culture that characterized his eventual five-decade involvement with the arts and peoples of Nigeria.

Kelly challenged the young priests to "establish a centre to study, among other things, the adaptation of African crafts to Christian uses and to experiment in this field."[6] The influence of Kelly's vision and the missionaries' own high hopes for their role as on-site art patrons can be felt in Carroll's later invocation of Abbot Suger, the famed French medieval mastermind of Gothic art and architecture. Carroll quoted art historian Émile Mâle on Suger, "'When iconography is transformed, when art adapts new themes, it is because a thinker has collaborated with the artists. Suger was one of these men who set art on new ways. . . . ' In our own smaller way, we tried to repeat the influence of Suger, although the full flower of African Christian art will require the guidance of African religious thinkers."[7] In pursuit of this Sugerian ideal, the workshop's patrons developed significant technical and cultural expertise in the areas of their greatest efforts, especially the articulate and scholarly Carroll. He subsequently published respected texts on Yoruba art (1967) and Nigerian architecture (1992) and numerous journal articles on Yoruba culture and inculturation topics for interested academics, church leaders and thinkers, and general readers in Europe and North America (see ch. 5).

The Workshop Artists

The workshop artists, recruited from the surrounding areas, certainly reflected their own ethnic Yoruba and Ekiti regional cultural influences. But as they also lived in a British colonial setting and were exposed to various sources of foreign imagery, such as packaging, other print media, and signs, they lacked immunity from the transmission of European visual culture. This was especially true of those local people who had gone through various levels of schooling in facilities usually run by Europeans and, often, missionary personnel. One of the definitive hopes spelled out by Kelly, that no European influences should shape the new art form, proved impossible to achieve, especially since the workshop's management was European and very new to the indigenization process. The considerable weight of centuries

SIDEBAR 4. THE OPIN-EKITI CARVING TRADITION

Yoruba art styles vary by community and location, and the main carvers of the Oye-Ekiti Workshop followed what is called the Opin style, after a collection of a dozen small villages currently in the state of Ekiti (see map, p. 4). This style is epitomized by the renowned carver Areogun of Osi-Ilorin (ca. 1880–1954), the last of a distinguished line of premodern carvers.

SB fig. 6. Carvers George Bandele and Lamidi Fakeye visit in George's old carving workshop. (David Curl)

Areogun's son, Bandele (1910–1995), the workshop's major carver from 1948 to 1954, was not trained by his father. Following a Yoruba proverb that declares that a child is spoiled by kindness in his father's house, Bandele was sent as a teenager to serve his apprenticeship in the home of Oshamuko of Osi-Ilorin, one of Areogun's former carving assistants. Carroll's book *Yoruba Religious Carving* [1] provided the first account of this tradition of carving in 1967, and John Picton deepened and expanded it in 1994, when he traced Opin carvers back to the early nineteenth century and diagrammed their interrelationships. [2] Both scholars document Bandele's carving technique in detail and provide the technical Yoruba terms for each phase of the carving process (see SB fig. 6). Lamidi Fakeye of Illa-Orangun (1925–2009) came from a nearby but different carving tradition in the Igbomina area near northwestern Ekiti. Not having served a true apprenticeship in his father's house, Lamidi agreed to serve a three-year apprenticeship under Bandele. [3] A pupil's work often resembles that of the master, and Lamidi's carving resembles Bandele's; he has also followed the Opin-Ekiti tradition, even through the development of the Neo-Traditional style in his later career. His nephew and former apprentice, Akin Fakeye has continued this style of carving. [4]

---

1. Carroll 1967.

2. Picton 1994c.

3. Lamidi et al. 1996, 99.

4. Fagg 1969, 53.

of Western European traditions of Christian representational art inevitably influenced the preferences and expectations of the patrons, especially as Carroll exercised both general and sometimes specific control over the artists' work.

Carroll recounts how the priests gathered local specialists in various branches of the traditional arts—carvers, weavers, embroiderers, potters, beadworkers, and leatherworkers—and began to organize and direct production.[8] Wood carving became the workshop's main area of artistic emphasis and fame due to a number of factors. In trying to adapt Christian content to an African culture, the workshop's Irish patrons, in the beginning certainly, reflected the Catholic clergy's dominant Eurocentric visual preferences and the requirements of the Church's ancient tradition of devotional statuary, relief, and other embellishments of ecclesial architecture, whether consciously or not.

By historical contrast, some Protestant religious practice, and especially that in the Calvinist tradition, which pursued austerity and forbade the use of pictures and sculpture, placed considerably less value on Christian artistic expression and consequently would have been quite reluctant to engage in such an experiment. In 1950, Kelly reemphasized the importance of an indigenous approach to religious expression, saying, "We ought not to substitute cheap foreign prints for native skill and culture; we ought to transform it and elevate it by Christianizing it . . . we cannot import (nor impose) minds, souls, culture, native genius. . . . We must develop what is there potentially."[9] In line with the mission's broader goals, that is, to develop self-help, initiative, and economic development in the community, the new missionary art patrons initiated brick making and tile making as well as supported traditional arts of weaving and carving, "to show the people they can help themselves."[10]

Though numerous, most artists in this collaborative relationship, other than the three most illustrious wood-carvers—Areogun, George Bandele Areogun, and Lamidi Olonade Fakeye—left behind little identifying documentation. Wide-ranging fieldwork has uncovered additional artists, however, and from their experiences, the outline of the workshop's functioning and its art production become more clear. In the opinion of academic specialists, the importance of artistic promise within the Yoruba expressive tradition that each individual brought to the experiment is a predominant, pragmatic trait of the workshop. And nowhere was Christian adherence or conversion to Christianity part of the patrons' calculations in the selection and hiring process.

George Bandele Areogun of Osi

As they began recruiting wood-carvers, the fledgling workshop and its neophyte patrons had the good fortune to be approached by an outstanding talent. George Bandele Areogun (1908–1995), of Osi-Ilorin, the son of a famous Yoruba carver, approached the patrons at Oye-Ekiti in late 1947. (Carroll rendered some names as they occur in the local Ekiti Yoruba dialect; this name is also written "George Bamidele Arowoogun" in standard Yoruba.) (See fig. 7.)[11] A traditionally trained wood-carver, he was known for being an ambidextrous and "accomplished artist, whose works could be found in the temples to the deities and the houses of the local nobility."[12] Bandele traveled the Ekiti region in pursuit of commissions, such as carved relief doors, but, with customary artistic opportunities meager, had become a victim of underemployment in the general decline of traditional patronage. In Carroll's estimate, the thirty-nine-year-old Bandele's technical skills, while great, had diminished because of inactivity, and the carver seemed eager to begin work in this experimental art form.[13] Picton, who later became well acquainted with both Carroll and Bandele, characterizes Bandele's initial condition as a loss of sculptural confidence in the face of a changing art market for traditional sculpture.[14] Unfortunately, we lack Bandele's own self-estimate, but in a short time, the carver began to reflect the high artistic potential sought by Carroll.

In a break with tradition and a step toward modernity, the workshop's mode of art production followed an approach uniquely its own and involved a conscious awareness by the artist and the patron (and later, the audience and clientele) of the constraints on expression. In discussing the workshop and so much else regarding Oye-Ekiti, the art historian frequently must depend on the patron's information and perspective, given the relative absence of the artist's voice in the written record, as in the following account.

While Bandele presented himself as a practicing Catholic to the workshop patrons, he appeared to be insufficiently educated in his new faith to carry out their general intentions.[15] An example of the widespread blend of cross-cultural and religious pluralism in the late colonial period, Bandele, (Carroll reported later in an unpublished draft article) continued to serve

Fig. 7. George Bandele Areogun of Osi-Ilorin, son of the renowned woodcarver Areogun, joined the Oye-Ekiti Workshop in 1948 and became Carroll's most reliable sculptor. He continued working with both Carroll and O'Mahony for decades after the workshop closed in 1954. (KCC)

as head of his local Ogboni society (a traditional religious-civic group composed of elders who wielded considerable local influence) yet also attended Catholic church on his own.[16] Bandele's first two attempts at pleasing his new patrons fell short of their expectations.

Carroll's account of Bandele's initial efforts to please his new clerical patrons illustrates the origins of the workshop's hybridized style and the relative influence of the patrons.[17] Carroll believed that the tactic he used with Bandele, of challenging the carver to attempt a Christmas Nativity set (the Holy Family and Three Kings), beginning with the Kings, was a successful catalyst. First, he asked Bandele to carve the Kings as traditional Yoruba *oba*, or kings, with one mounted in Yoruba veranda-post style, followed by the Holy Family in a less characteristically Yoruba style.[18] The missionaries encouraged Bandele to take a fairly literal approach to illustrating Bible-based stories, using Yoruba techniques and formal elements. Still fearing too much individual interpretation from the Yoruba artist, the patrons also recruited a well-versed Catholic parishioner to tell Bandele the particular story and then followed up personally with a discussion of specific details.[19]

In discussing a Yoruba-style portrayal of the Crucifixion with Carroll, Bandele suggested portraying Christ's corpus fixed to the cross with wood screws, replacing the biblically specified nails, since he believed screws were much stronger.[20] An experienced woodworker, Bandele clearly understood the qualities of various techniques involved in fastening a carved corpus to a wooden frame, but the patrons had not expressed their specific expecta-

Fig. 8. Crucifix from 1948, with a background of red beadwork by Jimoh Adetoye on the trunk and arms of the cross under Bandele's carved wooden corpus. Last seen in the International Exhibition in Rome, 1950–1952. (KCC)

tion of nails well and were quite hesitant to give the carver broad freedom to translate this central Christian icon. While Carroll cites this incident, which occurred in 1948, as an amusing anecdote explaining his patronly reluctance to allow very much exploration in these uncharted waters, his account also reflects the control that the missionaries preferred to exercise over Bandele's efforts and their inability to provide clear guidelines and priorities for the artist.

A crucifix Bandele made in that same year (see fig. 8)[21] presents an unusual detail: the "nail" head on the right has a visible crisscross groove, curiously similar to that on a Phillips screw head. This prompts the question of whether Bandele got his way after all, right under the patrons' noses. Today, whatever humor there is in this incident lies in Carroll's unfounded assumption that Bandele would instantly grasp even the finer points of the patrons' unexpressed or vague wishes. In practice, the patrons seem to have exercised cautious restraint upon him and other workshop artists in the unexplored reaches of their new Yoruba-Christian art, frequently relying on a literal biblical translation, which undoubtedly reflected the limits of their own developing notions of an appropriate degree of adaptation of Christian iconography into Yoruba visual culture.

Although representing a major boost in artistic collaboration, Bandele's presence among the Oye-Ekiti artists rooted the workshop within the region's art production tradition, as the patrons had hoped. A product of the traditional training system, Bandele had been apprenticed by his father, Areogun of Osi-Ilorin, a well-established and respected carver in the royal courts of the region, to one of his assistants, Osamuko.[22]

Not wishing to monopolize the workshop's assembled talent, Carroll and O'Mahony encouraged Bandele and all the artists to accept outside commission work in addition to expanding their own repertoires in the workshop's projects. Carroll continued to believe that these traditional art projects not only conformed to his order's goal of respecting and strengthening the local culture but also kept the artists linked to their local communities, the ultimate source of their artistic inspiration. And Bandele continued to carve pieces for traditional Yoruba religious, royal, and civic clients as well as for the Society of African Missions, which had begun collecting pieces of art reflecting Yoruba religious expression in Ekiti and from its other African mission centers for its museums in Europe and the United States (see appendix). Carroll also secured commissions for the carvers making copies of older sculptures so that the rare originals could be collected and preserved in the Lagos museum.

Areogun of Osi-Ilorin

In 1948, as Carroll promoted the integrity of the workshop's art and its practice of cultural adaptation, in addition to serving the order's conversion goals, he sought out Bandele's non-Christian father, the widely renowned Areogun of Osi (ca. 1880–1954) (figs. 9 and 10). This link with Areogun reflected the missionaries' (especially Carroll's) rejection of the typical European disregard of indigenous expression and their desire to deeply understand Yoruba visual culture as an integral part of their arts experiment. Over the seven years of the workshop's life, Carroll, who had developed the knack of drumming up outside commissions for all the artists, passed on many jobs to the distinguished elderly carver and his apprentices.

By 1952, accomplishing a veritable coup for the workshop's patronage of wood carving, Carroll finally talked the elderly carver into accepting an initial Yoruba-Christian project. And, not surprisingly, he did so in the same way he had introduced Bandele to the workshop's style, with a Christmas

Fig. 9 *(left)*. Areogun of Osi-Ilorin, one of the great premodern master sculptors, was introduced to Kevin Carroll, by his son, George Bandele Areogun. He eventually collaborated with the workshop and carved part of a Nativity set before his death in 1954. (KCC)

Fig. 10 *(right)*. Photographed in Orangun in 1949, this 1910 epa mask by Areogun focuses on a King, surrounded by wives and household, who wears a broad-brimmed crown with the okin bird, king of birds; the ears of mask are carved as horsemen. (KCC)

Nativity set. Areogun completed only the Three Kings before his death in 1954, bringing an end to this brief but promising collaborative effort.[23] Photographs in Carroll's archive reveal that Areogun carved the Three Kings in mounted positions, with two fashioned like the Yoruba rulers or military commanders that appear as equestrian figures on palace veranda posts or towering *epa* masks (see figs. 11 and 12).

A third figure depicts one of the Kings in the form of Eshu, the pipe-smoking *orisha* (Yoruba deity) (see fig. 13). The iconographic reference to Eshu as one of the Kings is proof of the workshop's commitment to cultural adaptation and some inevitable linking of Christianity with the local religion. The Eshu-type image introduces notions of ambiguity, resistance, and even humor in Areogun's pipe-smoking rendering of this unusual *oba*. We do not know Carroll's interpretation of this carved expression, nor that of

Fig. 11 *(left)*. One of the Yoruba-Christian Three Kings for a Nativity set carved by Areogun, his last piece of sculpture and currently in the possession of the Nigerian SMA. This mounted King is presented as an *oba*, or traditional Yoruba ruler, as often seen on *epa* masks. (NJB)

Fig. 12 *(right)*. A second King by Areogun, in the form of a mounted *oba* (traditional ruler) with a broad-brimmed crown. Its current whereabouts are unknown. Photo taken by Father Carroll in 1954. (KCC)

the artist, but Carroll usually left iconographic details to the carver. In earlier decades, other missionaries (including the Anglican Church Missionary Society) had sometimes crudely and erroneously equated this trickster *orisha* with Satan, the Judeo-Christian devil.[24] Clearly, Carroll's collaboration with Areogun ran counter to some strong and long-held biases within Yorubaland's Christian community. This limited association of an artist of Areogun's generation and stature clearly deepened the connection of the

Fig. 13. A third King from the set carved by Areogun. It displays some of the iconographic characteristics of the Yoruba *orisha* Eshu, illustrating the freedom of expression Carroll allowed artists at the Oye-Ekiti Workshop as part of the inculturation process. This figure is currently in the collection of the African Art Museum of the SMA Fathers, Tenafly, N.J. (NJB)

workshop and its artists and patrons with the illustrious past achievements of the Yoruba sculpting tradition.[25]

Lamidi Olonade Fakeye

Another Oye-Ekiti recruit, who arrived without fanfare, led the short-lived workshop to continuing international recognition. According to Carroll's recollection thirty years later, the workshop attracted an increasing flow of orders for its new artwork, such that by 1948, Carroll and Bandele felt financially able to take on an assistant.[26] After a number of tentative contacts, Bandele agreed to bring Lamidi Olonade Fakeye (1925–2009), a twenty-three-year-old from nearby Ila-Orangun (see map, p. 4), into the Oye-Ekiti workshop as an apprentice for three years (see fig. 14).[27] Lamidi was a fifth-generation member

Fig. 14. Lamidi Olonade Fakeye, who, as a young, untrained carver from a distinguished, five-generation carving lineage from Ila-Orangun, showed so much promise that Carroll agreed to have him serve a three-year apprenticeship in the workshop with Bandele in 1949. (KCC)

of a woodcarving lineage and believed he had been prepared through home-based training, but he had not yet served a proper Yoruba apprenticeship; instead, he had attended Catholic high school in Usi-Ekiti. Though Lamidi was relatively untrained, Carroll much appreciated his education, his carving lineage, and his interest in learning to carve professionally.[28]

On the issue of the artist's creative freedom under Oye-Ekiti patronage, Lamidi provides a good example of the relativity of the artists' religious point of view. Whereas Lamidi's wood-carver father, simply called Fakeye, practiced traditional Yoruba religion as an Ifa priest, Lamidi had become a Muslim as a teenager, while some other siblings espoused Christian beliefs. Speculating on Lamidi's enthusiasm for carving figures despite Islamic strictures against idolatry, Carroll later observed that few Yoruba Muslims actually accepted orthodox Islamic restrictions on three-dimensional representation and often syncretized local beliefs and Islam.[29]

Among traditional carvers, standard practice included carving for different Yoruba cult groups other than one's own. Lamidi's explanation, presented in his autobiography, relies on the justification that Solomon's temple had carvings on it, so his own practice of carving spiritual subject matter emulated the Scriptures.[30] In this complex level of artistic discourse, the indigenous artist may appear as a split personality or as merely serving a foreign art purpose out of self-interest. But, as Sidney Kasfir points out, "in pre-colonial patron-client interactions, it was the custom for artists to try openly to please patrons, even if this meant modifying form."[31] The expectations of the artists here do not seem out of line with Yorubaland precedent, and Lamidi's subsequent career success reflects the wisdom of his decision to join the Oye-Ekiti Workshop.

Bandele's approach to training Lamidi followed his own traditional apprenticeship, which had lasted three years and schooled him in the carving style of the northern Ekiti-Illorin border.[32] In a 1966 letter to John Picton, Carroll commented that Bandele recognized that he and his apprentice were appropriately separated by at least two age grades and preferred to go to the extent of performing a traditional initiation ceremony and ritual washing of the apprentice's tools.[33] Lamidi's own 1996 account of his introductory experience with Carroll's Nativity-set entrance assessment adds his perception of the situation and illustrates not only some of the difficulty of controlling cultural transmission of various types but also the artist's strong awareness of the differences between European and indigenous styles.

Bandele met Lamidi through a mutual acquaintance and later introduced him to Father Carroll, who, as a test of skills, according to Lamidi, "asked me to carve anything in my own style and bring it to the art workshop at Oye- Ekiti. . . . However, instead of carving a figure in my own style, I was hypnotized and thought that a European would like an English style and figure. . . . So I decided to carve an angel, which I painted in different colors."[34] When he returned with the finished work the following month, Lamidi continued, "Father Carroll did not even tell me whether the work was good or not. He just took it and (using an interpreter) asked me to come back anytime in March. . . . [Carroll then] gave me a commission to carve one of the three wise men of the Christmas story in white wood . . . so, since he had not rebuked me for the adulterated English style I had used before, I thought he preferred it . . . (and carved it) in the same style."[35] Through a translator, Carroll told Lamidi, "If I need carvings in a European style, I will look for them in England." He told the wood-carver that he could have a second chance but that his employment depended on his doing "something really African." Realizing that he was in danger of losing his new job, he wrote, "I crossed back to my original track [traditional Yoruba style]. . . . I recognized that my ideas were raw and could only be used advantageously if exposed and properly monitored" as Bandele's apprentice.[36]

Experiences like this one affected both sides of the collaborative relationship: Carroll and O'Mahony eventually became very fluent in modern Yoruba over the years of their deep personal involvement with the artists

Fig. 15. These four veranda posts were carved and painted by Lamidi Fakeye in 1954 for the palace of the prominent Yoruba ruler, the Ooni of Ife. Later, as faculty member of the University of Ife from 1992, Fakeye shows students his first independent commission of traditional Yoruba art forms, which he acquired through Father Carroll's efforts. (By permission of David Curl)

(in contrast to many European missionaries), and the artists, like Lamidi, learned to work closely with the patrons, to gain their trust and participate in the workshop's comparatively lucrative commission work. In his own estimation, Lamidi soon showed great improvement and gained commissions for outside projects (figs. 15 and 16), through both a growing recognition of his work and Carroll's constant promotion.[37] His reputation as a young, yet respected artist who reflected traditional carving practices eventually spread internationally, beginning with his visit to France and Great Britain and then to the United States in the 1960s. One of his proudest moments occurred late in his life, in 2008, when UNESCO and the Nigerian government honored him as a Living Human Treasure.

As to the carving styles of these three emblematic workshop carvers, one of the founders of both Nigerian and Yoruba art studies observed that the

Fig. 16. Lamidi's large, unpainted Yoruba *epa* mask is one of the traditional carving commissions that Carroll encouraged workshop artists to accept. Part of the Oye-Ekiti project's foundational idea was that artists should respect and preserve the art forms of Yoruba traditional religion and culture. This mask, honoring Osanyin, the *orisha* of healing, is now in the Kevin Carroll Art Collection, Dromantine, Northern Ireland. (NJB)

three carvers shared a common, almost familial, style. William Fagg, prominent curator at the British Museum, asserted that the strength of Areogun's forms was very apparent and his hand readily distinguishable throughout northern Ekiti.[38] He also noted that Bandele followed his father's style and that even the work of Bandele's apprentice, Lamidi, resembled the work of Areogun "at second remove." It has a "characteristic forehead line derived from Arowogun's own style," notable even in Lamidi's Christian work, here a crucifix.[39]

Other Artists of the Oye-Ekiti Workshop

Weavers, bead artists, and leather carvers were also present and fully involved in art development and production at Oye-Ekiti. Of great distinction was an

Fig. 17. The workshop's main bead artist, Jimoh Adetoye, known as Baba Ashileke (Father Beadworker), whose work is particularly evident in the sacred beaded crowns (*adenla*) worn by the Three Kings in the Exhibition Nativity sets and the tabernacle veils of that period. (KCC)

important bead artist and crown maker, Jimoh Adetoye (see fig. 17), known as Baba Ashileke (Father Beadworker), who resided at the workshop off and on for seven years. He was from Efon-Alaye, a member of a distinguished family of bead artists, and also continued to serve royal clients across the Ekiti region. As the workshop's senior beadworker, he produced textiles and many miniature crowns and garment designs for statuary. Carroll's 1967 account does not mention the role of dozens of textile workers, men and women, who helped produce various liturgical and market textiles that Carroll hoped would provide some income for the village, beyond the virtuoso work of the three or four prominent wood-carvers. A fortunate discovery in more recent years was the identity and contributions of the workshop's head woman weaver and tailor, Christiana Comfort Ajike Ojo. Other workers included embroiderers and leatherworkers between 1947 and 1954. In addition, Oye-Ekiti resident Joseph Ojo collaborated with Carroll in developing Yoruba-Christian music for devotional uses for many decades (also see Epilogue).

Jesus and the *Orisha* in Rome

During the early years of the workshop, from 1948 to 1951, Carroll and the workshop's master carver, Bandele, both separately and in collaboration, worked out some of the most significant ideas of their Yoruba-Christian fusion, which are reflected in a striking series of three Nativity scenes, all superficially similar, especially when viewed in the present. These scenes, which Carroll referred to as "Nativities," include figures of the Three Kings in the act of presenting their gifts to the Holy Family, and might more specifically be termed "Adorations of the Magi" or "Epiphanies." Viewed closer up and in chronological sequence, significant differences appear that graphically illustrate the workshop's earliest vision, challenges, and developing confidence as it proceeded on its bold path of experimentation and indigenization.

Three Challenging Nativities

Unfortunately, three significant early versions have been quite obscure in the workshop's spotty record until recent discoveries. Through archival research, fieldwork, interviews, and investigation of art collections in Nigeria, Ireland, and Italy (see Epilogue), I have been able to locate these Nativities and conduct a closer analysis. For convenience, I will refer to these three Nativities as follows: Nativity #1 is the 1948 Nativity, Carroll's own painting (see fig. 18); Nativity #2 is the 1949 Nativity, a carved set now in Rome (see figs. 19 and 20); and Nativity #3 is the 1951 Nativity, another carved set now in Assisi (see fig. 1). In this sequence, these pieces reflect the evolving private and public faces of this Yoruba-Christian collaboration during the crucial early stages of its path to Africanization.

Heralding the imminent international debut of the workshop's new art genre in 1950, Carroll published an illustrated article in *Nigeria Magazine*, then a colonial government publication, providing the first public introduction and a few of his photos of Yoruba-Christian art, notably of Nativity #2 (see figs. 19 and 20). In it, he recounts the request from the Vatican that the workshop send "examples of 'Sacred Art from the Missionlands' to a Holy Year Exhibition in Rome that year." The purpose of the exhibition was to unveil the latest results of the Church's policy of inculturation.[1] Surprisingly, his own book, published seventeen years later, does not contain even a single photo of these pieces, although Carroll did include one black-and-white image of a similar carved King from Nativity #3, perhaps because of its racial ambiguity.

In 1963, rare, high-quality professional photos of a second and very similar carved-and-clothed Nativity set, Nativity #3, appeared in full color, published by a small Catholic gallery in Assisi, Italy, although identified only as "Nigeria" (see fig. 2).[2] Other than these photographs in two obscure print sources, Nativity #2 and Nativity #3 dropped out of sight for almost half a century. Much more recently, in 2005, while continuing research in the Society of African Mission's Kevin Carroll Collection archive in Cork, I located a dated but unpublished color photo of an oil painting of a very similar Nativity scene (approx. 24 by 36 in.) done entirely by Carroll himself and dated 1948 by him (see fig. 18).[3] Unfortunately, the SMA does not know the current whereabouts of the painting, which was not among Carroll's effects at the time of his death in 1993.

A Yoruba-ized Painting

In Nativity #1, the earliest dated of the three Nativity images of the workshop era, Carroll, fully playing his role as Kelly's prototypical artist-missionary, exercises an artistic talent that he rarely displayed in public during his career as a missionary–art patron and scholar. He modestly characterized his talent as more like "drafting."[4] The painting presents the conventional Nativity scene that includes the Holy Family (Jesus, Mary, and Joseph) and the other subgroup, the Three Kings, as a completely African grouping (see fig. 18). The

Fig. 18. This 1948 Yoruba Nativity, painted in oil by Kevin Carroll, features the Holy Family and the Three Kings in a fully African Christian scene early in the Oye-Ekiti Workshop's development. Carroll, whose artwork is rarely seen, based his imagery on the local Ekiti sculpture he contually studied in the area. The whereabouts of this landmark painting, which suggests the ultimate path of indigenization Carroll's radical experiment was to take, are currently unknown. (KCC)

Three Kings appear as dark-skinned Yoruba *oba,* or traditional kings. The Holy Family is similarly dark-skinned but presented clothed in European Holy Family style, in full-length garments, and colored according to this convention. Mary is presented in a solid blue, full-length gown and a white veil, and Joseph wears a full-length brown tunic with cincture and carries an *apo Ifa,* a diviner's style carrying bag, on his shoulder, while the Christ Child wears only a loincloth or diaper. According to traditional Yoruba carving convention, young women were usually unclothed above the waist, but, not surprisingly, here Mary is fully clothed, emphasizing her maternal and married state. Carroll noted that the painting was "inspired by the work of Yoruba carvers and other craftsmen" with whom he was working and studying at the time.[5]

Carroll's Three Kings are clothed in the regalia of Yoruba *oba,* their heads covered by sacred beaded crowns, or *adenla,* and their robes made

Fig. 19. This Holy Family, carved and painted by Bandele, formed part of a significant Nativity set sent to Rome for the Vatican's 1950 Holy Year "Sacred Art from the Missionlands," an exhibition conceived by Archbishop Costantini as far back as 1940. Photographed by Carroll (later published in *Nigeria Magazine*) in 1950, his image and the accompanying article represent the world debut of the workshop's new Yoruba-Christian genre. The Holy Family figures of the Nativity set are missing but presumably still in Vatican City. (KCC)

from embroidered West African textiles. The Kings bear gifts for the new-born Christ Child, a variety of Yoruba carved offering vessels, at least one of which may be associated with Ifa, the Yoruba divinatory system. The vessels include a chalice-like cup supported by a bare-chested devotee and a bowl with a rooster-shaped lid. Most visibly, the Holy Family's skin color and other physical features are typically African as are those of the Three Kings. In this painted representation of the Holy Family, the artist creates a strongly Yoruba perspective by giving all of these central Christian figures a clearly African racial interpretation.

This grouping prominently features the Kings' gifts: The chalice-like vessel is very similar to a divination container, the *agere Ifa*, designed to hold the sixteen palm nuts that are cast on the *opon Ifa*, the divination tray, by a *babalawo*, or diviner. The bowl with the rooster-shaped lid, an *olumeye*, usually holds kola nuts, symbols of hospitality and generosity, and is used

Fig. 20. The Three Kings in this Exhibition Nativity set are dressed as Yoruba *oba* in sacred beaded crowns and rich West African textiles. They reflect an Early Modern European conception of the Kings as of mixed, non-European origins. In Carroll's conception, they appear vaguely non-European with the much darker central king presumably from sub-Saharan Africa. These three figures were recently located, identified, and photographed in the Pontifical Urbaniana University, Vatican City. (NJB)

in Ekiti and elsewhere to make offerings to the family for a child's naming ceremony or to prestigious visitors. Both kinds of vessels convey a significant visual suggestion, that Yorubaland's indigenous belief system provides fully worthy spiritual gifts for the Christ Child. The gifts named in the Gospel— gold, frankincense, and myrrh—have often been seen as prophetic symbols of Christ's life and death, and here Carroll provides the people of southwestern Nigeria with a vaguely parallel set of symbolic indigenous gifts for the Christ Child from the perspective of the Yoruba belief system. According to Africanist scholar of religion John Pemberton, the basic orientation of Yoruba divination sees that "the essential concern of every individual is to make one's way prosperously through life, drawing on the *ase* [spiritual power] of gods, ancestors, parents and nature to enable one to fully realize the personal destiny that he or she chose before coming into the world (*aye*)."[6] Through the process of divination, an individual discovers the nature of his or her own destiny. The significant Yoruba religious gifts in Carroll's Nativity #1 represent local parallels not only to gold, frankincense, and myrrh, but also to the prominent role of Hebrew Messianic prophecy in the Gospel account of the Christ Child.

A Nativity for Rome

In 1949, the year following his development of this fully Yoruba-ized Nativity painting, Carroll designed a second Nativity in collaboration with a small group of workshop artists in response to the Vatican's call for Christian art from the missions for the international exhibition in Rome for the Holy Year 1950 (see figs. 19 and 20). For Nativity #2, intended for a broad international public, he and a team of artists worked out a mixed-media ensemble of carved wooden figures in both fitted textile and painted garments. As in his Nativity #1, the Three Kings appear as local *oba,* wearing rich, tailored garments of woven and embroidered West African cloth and sacred beaded crowns. Often represented in early modern European paintings as exotic visitors from the East, these Kings wear formal *oba* regalia, which, due to British indirect colonial rule, was still quite prominent and recognizable in many southwestern Nigerian communities.

In Nativity #2, emphasizing the cultural distance between the Nativity's two subgroups, the Holy Family's garments are painted on the figures of Jesus, Mary, and Joseph in the conventional European Holy Family style. But the differences in skin tone between the two groups appear even more overt and telling. Members of the Holy Family are distinguished from the Kings by their lighter skin tone, although their physical features seem quite compatible with an African identity (see fig. 20).

Despite the clear prototypical direction of his earlier painting, Carroll apparently felt unwilling at this early point to advertise the full path of Africanization that the Oye-Ekiti experiment might be taking. Unfortunately, we lack any evidence of consultation with his colleague, O'Mahony, or others, on the decision to downplay or eliminate any racial affinity. Doubtlessly attempting to forestall a predictable Eurocentric, perhaps racist, reaction, Carroll even rejected the still inevitable African interpretation of the whole scene. In his *Nigeria Magazine* article, which includes the only contemporary photographs of the workshop's new Yoruba-Christian fusion, Carroll pointedly denies the Holy Family even a symbolic African identity: "She [Mary] is not painted dark as an African because everyone knows she was not an African but a Jew."[7]

Although not very clear in the old black-and-white pictures of the 1950 article, Nativity #2, destined for the Roman exhibition, presents the Kings with slightly different skin tones: two are moderately lighter, while one is very dark. These skin color variations have become quite clear, especially since the 2006 finding of the King figures in the Vatican's Urbaniana University (see Epilogue). By the 1960s, all the art from this Roman exhibition, including the Oye-Ekiti pieces, had dropped out of public view. Undoubtedly familiar with European Catholic images of this scene (the Adoration of the Magi), wherein the Kings are portrayed with different racial features, Carroll seems to reference these differences with the two varied skin tones.

After the exhibition closed in Rome in 1950, the collection traveled to the capitals of the two formally Catholic colonial powers, Spain and Portugal. A professor from the Urbaniana in Rome, Dino Satolli, who accompanied the show, wrote the catalogue for the last stop of the exhibition, in Lisbon in 1952. He comments on Oye-Ekiti's Virgin figure holding the Christ Child: "Her delicateness derived from the expression of love and care for her child." Satolli also observed that the Three Kings "are extremely beautiful in their fancy and festive clothing." He was struck especially by their facial expression, noting that "Their eyes, exceedingly large and pensive—unlike those of the other sculptures—seem to follow that 'dream,' the reason they pursue this route, following the star.... The most obvious reality comes from within and gives us the impression that they have not yet arrived at the stable in Bethlehem."[8]

The Cardinal's Nativity

The brainchild of Propaganda Fide's farsighted administrator, Archbishop (and later Cardinal) Celso Costantini, the 1950 "Exhibition of Sacred Art from the Missionlands" had become a showcase for the idea of cultural adaptation. After seeing the Oye-Ekiti Workshop's Nativity #2, Costantini, who was a noted art scholar and author in his own right, placed an order with the workshop for another carved and clothed Nativity set for himself, a signal honor for all involved. Finished and delivered to the cardinal in

1951, Nativity #3 (see fig. 2) eventually found a home in a small religious art museum in Assisi (see Epilogue). Years before locating either of these carved sets in Assisi and Rome, I came to rely on some full-color photos of Nativity #3 published in an obscure volume in Italian.[9] These professionally done color images allowed a good basis for comparison of the three sets, which became prime evidence of the path that the Oye-Ekiti inculturation experiment had taken.

In filling Costantini's order, the workshop naturally made the cardinal's set very similar to Nativity #2 in almost all respects. Nativity #3 presents a close likeness to Nativity #2, differing only in small ways. In Nativity #3, the Kings are dressed traditionally as *oba*, their skin is uniform in tone, and they carry prominent offering or divination pieces. As a group, they display a darker skin color than the Holy Family, a fact that Kevin Carroll was keen to highlight in his *Nigeria Magazine* article (i.e., that the Holy Family was *not* African). Because his painting of three years earlier portrayed the Holy Family with African skin color and features, Carroll apparently still did not judge the time appropriate for presenting a black Mary and Jesus to the Vatican and a broader international audience, or even to Cardinal Costantini, the person who had originated the idea and methodology of inculturation.

Neither party in this patronage relationship seemed to have a clear idea of the rules, pace, or limits of this new genre's evolution over time and struggled with it during the workshop's seven years and for decades after. Despite the existence of over fifteen hundred years of African Christian art in Ethiopia, the twentieth-century issue of representing Christ and Mary as dark-skinned Africans remained a contentious issue in various religious publications well into the 1960s, until the Second Vatican Council (1962–65) authoritatively signaled the Church's dominant view in support of inculturation in theory, thereby ending the official and public debate for Catholics. Carroll's own comments on the subject seventeen years later reflect his fully comfortable public acceptance of a clearly Africanized Jesus and Mary in the Yoruba-Christian public art he continued to patronize, commission, and promote.[10] Perhaps, by 1967, Carroll regretted his cautious approach to the issue of race in these early Nativity representations, which had scored so well with Costantini in 1950. When I interviewed Lamidi Fakeye in 2003, the workshop carver insisted that Father Carroll had always given the carvers great freedom in such matters.[11] Although the two exhibition Nativity sets express some caution, they certainly demonstrate the developing and boldly experimental approach the workshop fostered.

Early Mission Hostility

Raising the issue of racial identity in portraying the Holy Family both challenged and obscured another controversial issue also embedded in these Nativities. The harder and deeper question of the relationship of Christianity to indigenous religions in Africa and the rest of the non-European world continued to plague the usual encounters of missionaries and local populations. In early decades of mission work in Africa, the European missionaries knew little of the local culture, traditional values, and religious beliefs and frequently condemned much of them. Conventional missionary attitudes and practices rejected indigenous African art as the vehicle and handmaiden of "paganism." Moving to counter these missionary shortcomings, Costantini's idea of adaptation reversed this blanket rejection of the local cultures in the mission areas. Acceptance of local cultural elements was to be bounded only by vague papal strictures and, later, Vatican Council guidelines against cultural aspects "indissolubly bound up with superstition and error."[12]

While divination vessels might be easily dismissed as falling into this forbidden category, Carroll knew that Ifa, the Yoruba divinatory system, had a huge following, and not merely among adherents of traditional Yoruba religion. Ifa's sway also extended more broadly among neighboring ethnicities, sometimes in adjacent colonial territories, and also even among Muslim and Christian adherents in these areas. Carroll clearly perceived that a hostile missionary attitude toward the local religion not only prevented a full embrace of Yoruba culture in general, but also blocked a sincere appreciation of its closely related art forms. Scholars and observers soon realized that the links between Yoruba religion and the region's customary art forms were profound and that developing an appreciation for Yoruba art in general required more than a superficial awareness of the Yoruba belief system. Carroll's personal example illustrated the truth of this.

Relationship to Yoruba History and Religion

In the year the workshop closed, Carroll and Lamidi collaborated on a ten-panel double door for the Catholic chapel of the University of Ibadan, which

Fig. 21. Panel showing an early version of Carroll's Yoruba Transfiguration image, with Christ as the fulfillment of Yoruba (and Africa's) history. This is a panel on the double doors carved by Lamidi for the Catholic Chapel, University of Ibadan, 1954. (KCC)

included a sweeping image of Christ in glory (radiating light) flanked on the left side by the figure of a healer-diviner holding the staff of Osanyin, the *orisha* of healing, and on the right by the image of a northern horse rider holding a Qur'an board and prayer beads (see fig. 21). Similar to earlier horse-rider figures in Areogun's earlier panels, this Muslim figure symbolizes both the Hausa and the Fulani political and religious power prominent in northern Yorubaland since the late eighteenth century (see fig. 21). This 1954 panel centered on the Christ figure boldly presents Christ as the fulfillment of Yoruba history.

In the following years, Carroll formulated a more particular view of the importance of the customary Yoruba belief system. In two similar works of art, again by his close collaborator and carver Lamidi Fakeye, Carroll positions Yoruba traditional religion as extremely important, even foundational, to the relatively recently arrived (a century at most) Christianity. These works would be found in two prominent, Westernized urban settings. The first expression of this idea is in a carved panel for the back of the archbishop's throne, found in 1956, destined for the Catholic cathedral in the Oke-Padi suburbs of Ibadan, the Yoruba city of over eight million (see fig. 22). The second, found four years later, is a panel set just below eye-level on the carved, double front doors of a new church, St. Paul's in Ebute Metta, a neighborhood in Lagos, sub-Saharan Africa's largest metropolis.

Fig. 22. Carved back panel of the archbishop's throne in the Catholic Cathedral in Ibadan. It features Carroll's further development of a Yoruba Transfiguration, which places the Risen Christ between a Shango priest and a priest of Osanyin, implying that Christ fulfills the goals of Yoruba Traditional Religion. Carved by Lamidi Fakeye, 1959. (NJB)

An African Transfiguration

This newly developed image features three bare-chested male figures side by side. In the center appears a radiant, fully Africanized Christ figure with halo, arms opened wide, flanked by two other male figures, both facing in toward him. The figure on the left is a priest of the prominent *orisha* Shango, holding a full-length staff in one hand and an *ose Shango*, or Shango dance wand, identified by its double-headed thunder ax, in the other hand. The figure on the right is a priest of Osanyin, the *orisha* of healing, standing with his staves in hand. The haloed, short-haired figure of the risen Christ, with the wounds in his hands and side visible, wears local Yoruba garb, including a ceremonial skirt in the style of a Shango priest. In this booming urban center, where references to the *orisha* Shango would be widely recognized, Carroll continued to forcefully counter the once common Christian missionary enmity toward the traditional belief system by fashioning this African Transfiguration grouping.

The three synoptic gospels describe the Transfiguration as occurring shortly before Christ's return to Jerusalem for the last time. The term refers to the metamorphosis of Jesus into a radiant figure whom God identifies as the Messiah, the Son of God. In the Gospel account, Christ is joined at this high point of his brief public life by two significant personages from the Hebrew Scriptures, Moses and Elijah (or Elias). These two figures are often interpreted as symbolic indicators that Christ has come to fulfill the promises God made to the Jewish people, one being Moses, who represented God's gift of the Law, and the other being Elijah, who represented the gift of prophecy.

In this African adaptation, Christ becomes the fulfillment of the pre-

Christian belief system of the Yoruba peoples, not its opponent. The *ori-sha* Shango represents both a deity and a mythic ruler of the Oyo kingdom, who commands great power, as reflected in lightning and human fertility. Perhaps Carroll chose the popular Shango as a stand-in for Moses, since Genesis relates that when Moses went up to receive the commandments, he disappeared in a cloud accompanied by thunder and lightning. To represent the symbolism of the prophet Elijah, Carroll presents a priest of the religious healing system embodied in the *orisha* Osanyin. In this group association, Carroll parallels the relationship of Christ to Judaism with Christianity's relationship to Yoruba traditional religion, namely, seeing it as Christianity's worthy precursor, its forerunner, making the path in Yorubaland. While leaving the indigenous religion in a subordinate position, Carroll's image nevertheless stresses Christianity's continuity with the Yoruba religious past and sounds a note of fulfillment, not of opposition or condemnation.

The figures of King Shango and Osanyin the Healer suggest that Christ can be the source of security and healing, two significant ends sought by most African religions. The Catholic patrons and the religiously mixed local artists of the Oye-Ekiti mission, seeking to adapt Christianity to a Yoruba form of visual expression, hoped to pioneer a viable Yoruba art fusion and contribute to the continuing development of Yoruba culture. By mixing these three figures, Carroll and his coworkers hoped to set Christian religious content within the form of Yoruba traditional carving. O'Mahony, Carroll's longtime partner in this inculturation project, speaking later of the approach that the two missionaries took, asserted, "It's not that we want them to give anything up, but to add to what they have already."[13]

Anticipating criticism and opposition due to this radical shift in both perspective and representation, Carroll and his artists used powerful Yoruba imagery to present central Christian ideas in the process of becoming African ideas against a backdrop of colonial and religious Eurocentrism. Caution clearly slowed the development and introduction of the workshop's Africanized Christian genre. The relatively early date of Carroll's strongly Yoruba-ized 1948 Nativity painting proclaims the fullness of his personal commitment to his order's inculturation goals.

The significant contrast between this 1948 painting and the subsequent pair of carved sets made for the exhibition in Rome and Cardinal Costantini shortly afterward well illustrates the sensible caution he exercised, though the articulate priest did not directly mention it in his writings. The overt denial that he expressed in print in 1950 (that Mary is not African but a Jew) today seems strained and forced. In hindsight, this reluctance in expressing an African racial identity for the Holy Family needs to be balanced against his subtler, but nevertheless daring and public association of the Christ Child with the practice of Ifa divination, as evidenced in the gifts borne by the Kings. Nevertheless, Carroll knew that few, if any, observers in Rome would have recognized this bold assertion of the significant value of indigenous religion in his newly enlightened Christian reappraisal.

A Challenge to European Dominance

Since, in both words and deeds, Carroll's subsequent career represented an unambiguous statement of opposition to the widespread racist and Eurocentric attitudes and practices found in many pre–World War II colonial and ecclesiastical settings, I believe he may not have wished to revisit this early, quite understandable, though uncharacteristic compromise of his usually forthright cultural values. Partial downplaying of these values, not Carroll's preferred mode of approach, is not really inconsistent, given the circumstances of 1950, when such a compromise may have been necessary for the workshop's survival. He was later to write, "Yet, it is only by experiment, with its risk of failure and its part-successes, that a start can be made on the development of a modern [C]hristian art."[14] The unprecedented and undisguised mix of different religious traditions in comfortable association with each other reveals the dramatic shift in the Christian art that Kelly, Carroll, and O'Mahony produced at Oye-Ekiti; these early works virtually assured a serious reaction from within the Church community. As confidence developed, the workshop grew bolder, and the Yoruba Transfiguration panels from the next decade indicate a more comfortable and unambiguous pairing of the local culture with Christianity in their deep embrace of Yoruba traditional culture, even more so than Carroll's early Nativity painting, although the sheer visual appeal of the exhibition sets, with their three richly clothed and crowned Kings and their suggestion of Ifa divination, is undeniable.

In confronting the issue of the racial and cultural identities of Christ and other Gospel figures, Carroll challenged that aspect of Christian expansionism that had idealized European cultures and their imperialism as the primary vehicle for the "universal goal of winning all nations for Christ."[15] As detailed in J. D. Y. Peel's important study "Ethnogenesis of the Yoruba People,"[16] "Christian missionaries contributed substantially to the emergence of nationalism through the introduction of Western education, social reforms and political ideas."[17] In the years leading up to national independence, the workshop progressively resisted the imposition of European visual expression and its concomitant denigration of local culture, including the indigenous religion, in the Nigerian mission context. The SMA's Oye-Ekiti scheme aided in rectifying and balancing the tendency within Christianity of specific groups (e.g., Europeans) to feel specially "commissioned" to carry the Gospel. Conceptualizing, collaborating, and creating African Christian images reflected a strong reaffirmation of the universality of Carroll's and Kelly's Christian message. Unfortunately, such Eurocentric tendencies died slowly.

Beyond the Workshop

In this initial period following its formulation and promotion by Cardinal Costantini in the 1930s, implementation of inculturation in the visual arts proved controversial within the Church, particularly in southwestern Nigeria, despite Carroll's caution and the many positive comments from Vatican leaders, sympathetic British colonial figures, and a growing international clientele for Oye-Ekiti's art production.[1] The archive bears clear evidence that Carroll faced pronounced opposition to the experiment from many, including the Church hierarchy, indigenous and missionary clergy, laity, and even local college students—the future educated Christian elite in Nigeria. This wider resistance to the Yoruba-Christian experiment is reflected in the critical comment made in 1954 by an older monsignor, one of the first generation of Yoruba Catholic priests: "Are you trying to take us back to what we have left?"[2] Clearly, some Yoruba Catholics associated the new genre with traditional Yoruba art, which early missionaries sometimes stringently rejected as the partner of the frequently demonized traditional religion.

Workshop Closure

The workshop's founder and mentor, Dr. Patrick M. Kelly, was not renewed in his term as leader of the Irish Province of the Society of African Missions in 1952. The circumstances that led to this decision included growing opposition within the Irish Province against Kelly's more Africa-centered mission policies, including the workshop, which, it was argued, had led to neglect of his other areas of responsibility. Some of his confreres in Ireland complained that the visionary provincial spent too much time and money in the field and not at SMA headquarters in Ireland, taking care of the province's administrative and financial details. By 1954, a newly installed provincial superior ordered the workshop closed, on the grounds that it was no longer financially viable and was an unacceptable drain on SMA funds. He did, however, encourage Carroll and O'Mahony to carry on with their Yoruba-Christian experiment with a lower profile at separate new assignments in Nigeria. Carroll always maintained that the workshop had become self-sufficient and provided ample evidence of orders and receipts in its records. Clearly, there were additional factors in the decision to close the scheme. The Nigerian hierarchy (composed at that time almost exclusively of European missionaries) backed off its early tentative support for the radical art project, yet decades later, it would bemoan the lack of cultural specialists in the Church who could advance multiple inculturation projects.

Despite its short life, the Oye-Ekiti Workshop locates a confluence of several major currents of twentieth-century African history: the political transformation of Nigeria and its peoples from European colonialism to national independence and the religious transition of Nigerian Christianity from a foreign mission history to an indigenous church history. The workshop also evokes themes of world history in its broader context: the large-scale adoption of Christianity in Africa as a significant part of the globalization of Christianity (and Catholicism) and the geopolitical shift of the preponderance of Christianity from the Northern to the Southern Hemisphere. Finally, for historians of African art, Oye-Ekiti marks a transition of the customary arts of Yorubaland in the development of both a Neo-Traditional Yoruba art and its sibling genre, the Yoruba-Christian hybrid, at the very root of the origins of contemporary Nigerian art.

Beyond the Workshop, a Nigerian Setting

The workshop's demise in 1954 redirected Carroll, O'Mahony, and the SMA's inculturation program from the countryside to broader, sometimes urban settings and even beyond Yorubaland. This important transition paralleled an expansion of Carroll's artistic and cultural perspectives within the larger context of the national Independence period in Nigerian history. No longer set in rural isolation, Carroll's post-workshop vision of an indigenized Christian art embraced a greater, fermenting mix in the new Nigeria, a nation with the largest multiethnic population in postcolonial Africa. Carroll's consultation on the St. Paul's Church project in the sprawling metropolis of Lagos, Nigeria's (and sub-Saharan Africa's) largest city, significantly redirected his thinking out of the rural, traditional, colonial, and exclusively Yoruban context of the workshop period and into a more contemporary and pan-Nigerian national panorama.

After leaving the Oye-Ekiti site, the two missionaries and their leading carvers, George Bandele and Lamidi Fakeye, continued their collaboration in a decentralized fashion, though without the vital synergy and momentum of the workshop setting. Lamidi followed O'Mahony to Ondo, and Bandele continued working with Carroll in Ijebu-Igbo and subsequent postings. Extensive correspondence and numerous receipts in the archive indicate that Carroll continued to promote the collaborative development, commission, and sale of Yoruba-Christian artwork both within the expanding Nigerian Catholic and Anglican communities and to an increasing international clientele in Europe, Britain, and the United States.

Non-Christian Work

From the time of its inception, the Oye-Ekiti scheme envisioned artists continuing to provide artwork for outside clientele, especially the royal courts and local *orisha* shrines, their traditional sources of patronage. This non-Christian work deserves significant attention (see figs. 15 and 16). Carroll tried to draw a line between the artwork the workshop provided directly for Yoruba traditional religious purposes (which he forbade) and work that the carvers agreed on their own to supply. Kelly, O'Mahony, and Carroll maintained as one of their foundational principles that workshop artists should continue some traditional Yoruba art production in order to keep up their skills, remain connected with their cultural roots, and help in the preservation of traditional arts and crafts in the region.[3]

Throughout the rest of his life, Carroll continued his patronage of the Yoruba-Christian genre, cultivating younger artists as well as providing Bandele, Lamidi, and others with a small but steady flow of commissions for church doors, baptismal fonts, screens, statuary, crucifixes, and devotional pieces (see figs. 23, 24, 26–30). Continuously balancing religious purity with the desire to promote the workshop's artists, their livelihood, and their cultural connections, Carroll favored the interests of his artist-collaborators.

Fig. 23. Lamidi Fakeye standing in front of his intricately carved double doors, centrally placed in the front of St. Paul's, in the Ebute Metta suburb of Lagos. This church embodies Kevin Carroll's expanded vision of an indigenized Nigerian Christian art. (David Curl)

He welcomed commissions for pieces such as monumental *epa* masks from sources that promoted mission art and activities, such as the museums of the SMA provinces in Europe and the United States (see Appendix), whereas the carvers handled commissions from traditional religious groups without the involvement of the patrons (see fig. 25). After he left the workshop, and when he was better known among colonial officials and others, Carroll also began passing along commissions from secular and civic sources to artists he knew.

Lamidi and Neo-Traditional Carving

With Carroll's firm support, Lamidi received more frequent commissions from governmental agencies and institutions, such as hospitals and universities, which eventually provided public and secular sources of patronage. As he moved beyond Carroll's patronage during the 1960s, Lamidi took on appren-

Fig. 24 *(above left)*. A Yoruba-Christian baptismal font, the form based upon the large Ogboni society drum *(agba)*, carved by Bandele for the church in Ondo. Includes the Risen Christ and a Shango priest. (NJB)

Fig. 25 *(above center)*. Bandele's carved drum for a Yoruba Ogboni society, of which he was a member, despite his adherence to Catholicism. It provided a model for many of the workshop's baptismal fonts, as seen in fig. 24. (KCC)

Fig. 26 *(right)*. Bandele's towering wooden image of Mary, Mother of Us All. The form reflects the tall, crowded superstructures of some monumental *epa* masks that are also carved from a single section of tree trunk. (NJB)

tices, opened his own studio, and subsequently visited France, Britain, and the United States for lecture-demonstration tours at many universities and museums.[4] Having laid the foundation for an impressive international career, Lamidi began exhibiting and selling his smaller carvings in Ibadan and eventually moved to the booming Yoruba metropolis in 1962. There, this pupil of Bandele, trained in the Opin-Ekiti carving tradition and descended from an illustrious line of carvers from Ila-Orangun, began building a new international practice, based on a clientele of foreign, mostly American, visitors. This new market was made up of people who, while interested in the older Yoruba carving styles, preferred smaller, more portable pieces that could be packed in suitcases and taken home as souvenirs of time spent in Nigeria, and often worked for agencies like the Peace Corps. Notable among Lamidi's early encounters with Americans was that with Isabel Beeler, wife of an American professor from Western Michigan University, then working with the U.S.

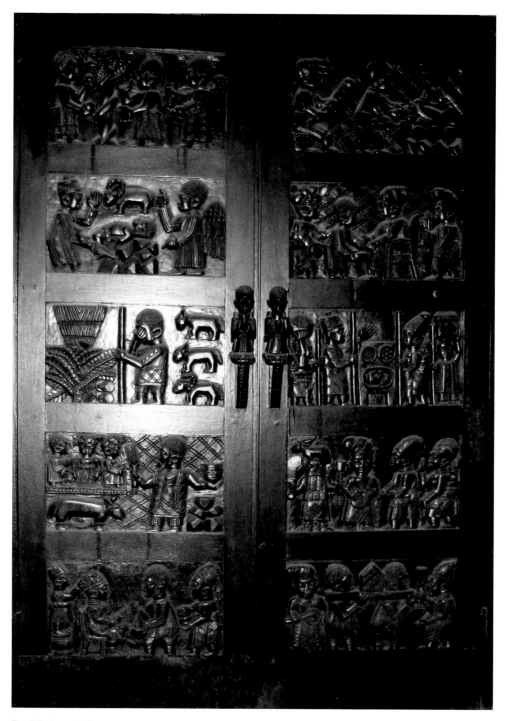

Fig. 27. Bandele's double, carved panel doors, now painted and still in use, in the Catholic Chapel of the University of Ibadan. (NJB)

Fig. 28 *(left)*. One of four sides of a tabernacle veil, each illustrating diferent images of the Tree of Life, ca. 1950. The beadwork and embroidery are likely by workshop artists, Jimoh Adetoye and Christiana Ojo. This veil and three others are in the Kevin Carroll Art Collection. (NJB)

Fig. 29 *(right)*. A beaded tabernacle veil modeled on the *Adenla*, the sacred beaded crown of an *oba*, a Yoruba ruler, surmounted by bird figures which represent the power of elder women in supporting the community. (NJB)

Agency for International Development in Nigeria, who had seen and appreciated his recent veranda-post carvings. Beeler counseled Lamidi to adapt his work to this more portable style in order to pursue this new audience.[5] This development in his carving has come to be termed Yoruba Neo-Traditional carving (see Sidebar 5, "Yoruba Neo-Traditional Carving").

Lamidi continued to carve and exhibit internationally in the closely related genres of Yoruba Neo-Traditional and Yoruba-Christian carving. In 1978, he combined his carving projects with a long period as an instructor in the art department of Obafemi Awolowo University in Ife (see figs. 31 and 32). For more than forty years, a growing community of wood-carvers gathered in Ibadan, founded workshops, and trained apprentices, most of whom were relatives and others trained by either Lamidi or his master, George Bandele, who died in 1995 (see fig. 33). Lamidi continued to carve and dem-

Fig. 30. One of Lamidi's last Christian works, carved in 2007, this Annunciation panel depicts the story in the Gospel of Luke I:2638 (and also in Lamidi's Qur'an, surah 3). The scene shows the Angel Gabriel (Jebril) informing the young Virgin Mary (Maryam) that, by God's will (symbolized by a dove as the Holy Spirit), she miraculously will conceive a child, Jesus. In portraying Mary as a rural Yoruba teenager performing a common household chore of pounding yams, the panel demonstrates that, although much of Lamidi's later fame was based on Neo-Traditional creations, he still liked to carve in the Yoruba-Christian genre that the Workshop had created six decades earlier. (NJB)

onstrate his Neo-Traditional carving techniques internationally as they have evolved through a long and productive career approaching six decades, until his last visit in 2009 to a dozen American campuses (see fig. 34). Clearly, it is because of the Oye-Ekiti Workshop and Carroll that the premodern Yoruba carving tradition survives today through Lamidi's relatives, associates, and pupils (see SB figs. 8 and 9).

Church Design and St. Paul's

Besides playing the lead role in developing the Yoruba-Christian genre, Carroll also expanded his efforts and perspectives to meet the challenge of constructing indigenously influenced Christian sacred space in Nigeria around the period of Nigerian independence. Once out of the workshop context, Carroll found himself increasingly involved in the larger issues of inculturation and church design, perhaps the ultimate development of his work, although he lacked specific architectural training. In his first posting after the workshop closure, he worked as the traveling religion resource for the schools of the Archdiocese of Lagos, from 1954 to 1962. During this time, he again consulted with architect Maxwell Fry on the furnishing of the Catholic Chapel of the University of Ibadan (1954), and, beginning in 1956, he collaborated with Father Harry Sheppard, SMA, in the building and furnishing of St. Paul's Church in Ebute Metta, a large suburb of Lagos.

Figs. 31–34 *(clockwise from upper left):*

Fig. 31. Independent artist Lamidi Fakeye promotes some of his popular Neo-Traditional pieces carved for an American exhibition in 1987. (David Curl)

Fig. 32. Lamidi Fakeye, age eighty-two, with the wooden monument he carved of Oduduwa, a Yoruba *orisha* and legendary founder of the Kingdom of Ile-Ife and all Yoruba civilization. Located at Obafemi Awolowo University in Ife, where Lamidi worked and taught in the art department from 1978 until his retirement. (NJB)

Fig. 33. Lamidi, the former apprentice carver, visits George Bandele, his former Workshop-era master in 1992 in Bandele's home town of Osi-Ilorin. (David Curl)

Fig. 34. On his last tour of the United States in 2009, Lamidi carefully demonstrates his art of wood sculpture at Hope College in Holland, Michigan, one of his favorite American venues, just two months before his passing. (NJB)

SIDEBAR 5. YORUBA NEO-TRADITIONAL CARVING

Yoruba Neo-Traditional sculpture is descended from the non-Christian carving work that Carroll commissioned from the workshop's carvers for interested collectors or that the artists accepted from more traditional clientele on their own time. By the late 1950s, Carroll had assisted Lamidi in putting together one of his first exhibitions, helping the young artist to develop the confidence to strike out on his own.[1] When Lamidi Fakeye, who was trained by Bandele in the Opin-Ekiti style, left Carroll's patronage and established himself as an independent master carver in the early 1960s, he began generating a whole new patronage centered in and around Ibadan. Through his foreign contacts, Lamidi pursued broader exposure with an international career, thereby promoting the fame of this new genre in the coming decades. His work can be seen today in the collections of many public art and educational institutions, including a set of door panels in the Africa Room of the John F. Kennedy Center in Washington, D.C.

The new expatriate and Nigerian middle-class clientele supported not just Lamidi but also his former apprentices and relatives, many of whom he had trained,[2] as well as other carvers who also sculpted in generally the same style. In researching this art form in Nigeria, I visited Ibadan in 2006 and met carvers following in Lamidi's footsteps, such as his nephew and former apprentice, Akin Fakeye, who works in a style derived from Lamidi and his artistic predecessors, Bandele and Areogun, sculpts both Neo-Traditional and Yoruba-Christian figures (see SB figs. 7 and 8). Also continuing in this style of carving is the coordinator of the Oyo State Carvers Association, Dick Idehen. A carver himself, Idehen ran a stand in Ibadan selling the works of the group's members. Decades after its early artistic lineage, the Opin-Ekiti style, dwindled following Areogun's death in 1954, Yoruba Neo-Traditional carving remains a viable art practice (see SB fig. 9).

---

1. Fakeye et al., 109–110.

2. See John Picton 2002, 100–101, and Day 1999. "Recent Wood Carvings in Idaban: Some Observations," *Nigerian Field* 64 (April): 3-27.

SB fig. 7 *(top left)*. Akin Fakeye, nephew and former apprentice of Lamidi Fakeye, and his two sons run a carving studio in Ibadan, where they sculpt both Neo-Traditional and Yoruba-Christian pieces. (NJB)

SB fig. 8 *(top right)*. Yoruba-Christian carvings of the Three Kings by Akin Fakeye and his sons in 2006. (NJB)

SB fig. 9 *(bottom left)*. Dick Idehen, chairman and organizer of the Oshun State Carvers Association, with Sunday Ayoola, a fellow carver. They are tending a consignment shop in Ibadan that offers Yoruba Neo-Traditional sculpture carved by some of the association's dozens of members. (NJB)

The university chapel became the first Catholic church in Nigeria to be built in a contemporary international style, utilizing "pre-cast concrete units for screen-work walling between the main structural forms."[6] From the beginning, both of these churches envisioned the use of Africanized Christian art.

With St. Paul's Church, Carroll mentions a degree of popular resistance to some of the African elements that he and Sheppard included in their plans for its design, construction, and furnishing, notably the "Arabesque patterns, derived from Hausa mud-wall decoration in northern Nigeria" on

Fig. 35. Kevin Carroll's photo of St. Paul's Church in Ebute Metta, Lagos, 1960, featuring
the Hausa mud-wall style design he had observed in northern Nigeria. The pattern is
a highly visible marker that this church was intended to reflect the whole of the newly
independent Nigeria and not simply the artistry of Yorubaland. (KCC)

the church's front, which, as a local wisecrack asserted, made the church look
like a mosque (see fig. 35).[7] In 1961, a side altar niche featured a large, wall-
mounted African Madonna by Paul Osagie Osifo, a carver from Benin City,
and Carroll records that Sheppard and his supporters on the parish building committee patiently worked to overcome the parishioners' objections to
African images based on their similarity to "pagan carving" (see fig. 36).[8]

The following year, a similar reaction arose when the carved panels by
the increasingly sophisticated carver Lamidi Fakeye were installed on the
great front double doors (see fig. 23). As mentioned, these doors included one
of the earliest versions of Carroll's Yoruba Transfiguration design. Carroll
noted again that there was some logic to the critics' complaints that this was
the same type of image "which the priest had made them reject when they
became Christians."[9] But later the same year, his installation of a baptismal
screen by Yoruba carver Otooro of Ketu produced "little vocal opposition"
(see figs. 37 and 38).[10]

A few years later, in 1967, the Lagos-based Urhobo painter, sculptor, and
graphic artist Bruce Onobrakpeya, an Anglican Christian from Delta State,

Fig. 36 *(left)*. This African Madonna, mounted on a wall in a side chapel at St. Paul's, was carved in 1961 by Benin City carver Paul Osagie Osifo. It evoked some vociferous opposition among a faction in the congregation. Carroll relates that the pastor and members of the church's building committee responded that "the Church in Africa must boldly tackle the work of producing her own Christian art." (Carroll 1967, 133) (KCC)

Fig. 37 *(right)*. The intricately carved-through and colorfully painted Baptismal screen of multiple panels with Christian subjects by Otooro, a sculptor with traditional beliefs from among the Ketu Yoruba in eastern Nigeria and Dahomey (now Benin Republic). (NJB)

agreed to create paintings of the Stations of the Cross—commemorating Christ's passion and death—for the church. A 1962 graduate of the new art college in Zaria (now Amadu Bello University), he was part of a group of innovative artists, the Zaria Rebels, which included Uche Okeke and others of a new generation of artists of the early Independence period. Onobrakpeya was teaching at St. Gregory's College in Lagos, where he happened to meet Carroll's brother, Patrick, also an SMA priest, who provided the connection for this first commission, which led to many subsequent projects, including illustrations for the New Nigerian National Catechism (1968).[10] A true success story of early Church patronage, Onobrakpeya was able to set himself up as an independent artist with his own studio in the 1970s, leading to a successful, internationally recognized art career.

The young artist and his assistants installed high on the walls of St. Paul's the series of fourteen large paintings (ten by four feet) featuring familiar bib-

Fig. 38 *(top)*. The First Station of the Cross, Pontius Pilate condemns Christ to death, by Bruce Onobrakpeya, 1967. Figures are portrayed in contemporary Nigerian dress, with Pilate as an *oba*, Christ in Christian clerical habit, and the soldier in colonial police–style uniform. (NJB)

Fig. 39 *(middle)*. The Fifth Station of the Cross, Simon of Cyrene carries the cross for Christ, by Bruce Onobrakpeya, 1967. Yoruba *adire* cloth patterns are used on the surfaces of Simon's clothing, on the cross, and for the background. (NJB)

Fig. 40 *(bottom)*. The Sixth Station of the Cross, Veronica offers her veil to wipe Christ's face, by Bruce Onobrakpeya, 1967. *Adire* patterns cover the cross, background, and Veronica's dress wrap and head-tie. (NJB)

lical scenes in a modern-day African setting, with the individuals depicted in a late colonial style, Roman soldiers garbed in colonial police–style uniforms, and indigenous *adire* textile patterns covering various surfaces (see figs. 38–40). Again, the St. Paul's parish community was divided on this nonhistorical portrayal of crucial Christian subject matter. In his important volume on Yoruba art, published in 1967, Carroll optimistically speculated that the novelty of African art in church had worn off and that the roots of the opposition lay in the unfamiliarity of the style.[11]

Chapels in the Middle Belt

From 1977 to 1982, Carroll took an assignment outside of Yorubaland, in Papiri and Guffanti in North Kwara State (see fig. 41). Here he eagerly accepted the challenge of designing and building two entire chapels according to his current ideas of inculturation, this time within a different cultural context, that of the Kamberi people of Nigeria's Middle Belt. Carroll's thinking at this time is distilled in the draft of a short article he wrote for the German liturgical periodical *Kunst und Kirche* in 1981, "Nigerian Christian Architecture."[12] In it, he observes, "In the Catholic Church, priests and people plan the largest possible building within their resources, and no consideration is given to small family or community shrines," as are found among Muslim and traditional religious groups, noting that even a large church often could not accommodate the community for the big feasts—Palm Sunday, Christmas, Holy Week, and Pentecost.[13] He favored the planting of a grove of fast-growing trees near or in front of the church as a realistic solution for these special overflow occasions.

In the article, he expressed a more personal interest, suggesting the advantages of the small decorative chapel or shrine. New Christian communities, which often had only temporary churches, not fully enclosed and with thatched roofs, could build small shrines for "weekday masses, for reserving the Blessed Sacrament, for baptisms, etc."[14] He also favored the idea of a family or local shrine for daily prayer and an occasional Mass.

These views reflected his current project, a pair of chapels built in the local style of the area. One, a shrine-chapel near his parish house in Guffanti, had begun construction in 1977, and the other, a small chapel next to a convent in Papiri, was initiated a few years later. He observed that the local Kamberi lived "in scattered households, not villages, throughout the bush," and consequently did not yet need a large church. They held prayer services

Fig. 41. A rare photograph of Father Carroll and local children in a community located to the north of Yorubaland in the Borgu area of Nigeria's Middle Belt. (KCC)

in people's homes or under shady trees, something analogous to indigenous sacred groves.[15]

Construction on the two chapels began with stone and concrete for the foundations and concrete for the floors. The walls and roofs were made with local materials, including mud for the walls and grass and timber for the roofs. The concrete and other "modern" materials were used in order to combat the natural enemies of mud and thatch, namely, rain and termites (white ants), and insecticides were applied around the foundations.

According to Carroll's concise descriptive notes on the first chapel in Guffanti: "The mud walls slanted in toward the top and were made rain resistant with the traditional rendering of a brown gum, made from the pods of the locust-bean tree (called *makuba*). Later, I found that some peoples in the Plateau area were using engine oil instead of *makuba*. It soaked into the walls and produced much the same rich brown appearance as the *makuba*, but lasted much longer."[16] (See figs. 42 and 43.)

Carroll based the decorated wall behind the sanctuary on the interior decoration of the northern Hausa people. He used their technique of mold-

Fig. 42. Guffanti chapel, exterior, North Borgu, designed by Fr. Carroll in Nigeria's Middle Belt, 1978. (KCC)

Fig. 43. Guffanti chapel, interior, altar wall, 1978. (KCC)

Fig. 44. Local mud artist Enugu Kagbaari collaborated with Fr. Carroll on the altar decoration in the Kamberi style at the Guffanti chapel. (KCC)

Fig. 45. Guffanti chapel door, close-up, 1978. Joseph Agbana, Carroll's favorite Yoruba carver in later years, created panels on the familiar Gospel themes but with a broader range of Nigerian ethnicities present, especially those of the Middle Belt region. Note the Nigerian Transfiguration panel at the lower right. (KCC)

Fig. 46. Father Carroll shows carver Lamidi Fakeye the entry to the Guffanti chapel by fellow-carver Joseph Agbana. (David Curl)

Fig. 47. Papiri hospital chapel interior, 1984, designed by Fr. Carroll with indigenous artists; the interior was Kamberi, but the exterior more in the Nupe style, according to Carroll. (KCC)

ing patterns on the wall with a mixture of earth and cement and then fixing flakes of mica on the wall with gum to produce a glittering gold effect. The tabernacle niche and another niche in the west wall for cruets and other altar vessels were influenced by the wall niches of the Nupe people (see fig. 43). Egunu Kagbaari, a local artisan, decorated the stone-and-mud altar in the Kamberi fashion (see fig. 44). The posts at the entrance and the door were carved by Yoruba artist Joseph Agbana, of Inisha (Oshun State), who also carved the Madonna for the interior of the church (see figs. 45 and 46). Long raffia mats covered the cement benches. Carroll mentions in his notes that this little chapel could hold about fifty people.[17]

The second, smaller chapel was built for the Sisters of Our Lady of the Apostles, a missionary community associated with Carroll's Society of African Missions, which ran a small hospital composed of a clinic and maternity ward at Papiri (see fig. 47). Similar in construction to the Guffanti chapel, this exterior struck him as more Nupe in style, especially notable in the windows and the entrance.[18] He also had the front walls decorated with patterns scratched into the wet cement, Nupe style. The interior (sixteen by twenty feet) he describes as Kamberi style, the walls plastered with black mud and patterns incised using a smooth stone. Again, Kamberi artist

Egunu Kagbaari made the more complex moldings behind the altars, and the Yoruba-Christian–style statues placed in the wall niches behind the altar came from the workshop of carver Joseph Agbana (see fig. 52).

After his work on these two chapels, if someone suggested that churches be built of earth in a "traditional" manner, Carroll's response was to insist that this was not what people wanted: they were not "going to wear their best clothes on a Sunday morning only to have them spattered with mud."[19] He notes the regular maintenance both chapels required, advising that even commercial resin coatings need refreshing every two or three years. In "Chapels in North Borgu," an unpublished 1991 article, he stresses: "These partly traditional chapels are difficult to maintain by anyone not familiar with the technique and materials. However, they give a good idea of what could be done in larger churches using modern materials and techniques, but influenced by traditional cultures."[20]

Carroll's Later Career

In summary, Carroll bluntly asserted that there were very few chapels and no churches with a distinctive Nigerian style, but there were many that incorporated Nigerian art. Throughout the rest of his life, he continued his patronage of the Yoruba-Christian genre of liturgical arts (including music) and architecture, cultivating younger artists and acting as an articulate advocate for inculturation into the early 1990s. His continuing patronage, promotion, and inspiration provided carvers Bandele, Lamidi, Bruce Onobrakpeya, Joseph Agbana, and other artists with a small but steady flow of commissions for church art and architectural elements.

In his 1981 article on Nigerian church architecture, Carroll pointed out one major difficulty in the employment of Nigerian artists, craftsmen, and builders: "Many priests . . . feel unqualified to direct the artists themselves, and I can only handle a fraction of the work that is wanted. . . . It is fortunate that one Mission Society made a serious initiative in this field," a final reference to the farsighted project begun by Father Kelly and two young artist-missionaries more than sixty years ago.[21] The "new kind of missionary" Kelly had thought of seemed more in demand than ever.

In January 1993, at the age of seventy-three, Kevin Carroll died from complications of an injury to his foot after a short illness. His funeral was attended by a dozen, mostly indigenous Nigerian bishops and archbishops, as well as more than a hundred priests. A telling comment on Father Carroll, written by his longtime friend and collaborator from Oye-Ekiti, musicologist Joseph B. Ojo, came fittingly in the form of a traditional Yoruba *oriki*, or praise song, performed by Ojo's children's choir from Oye-Ekiti at the requiem Mass in Ibadan. The following excerpts epitomize the hopes and values that animated the missionaries who were involved in the Oye-Ekiti experiment, and no one more than Kevin Carroll:

> In the month of November last year I was with you at Ilorin.
>
> "I am becoming old," said Kevin Carroll.
>
> I asked him when he would like to go back to his hometown.
>
> "What shall I go there to do?" said Carroll. "Who knows me in my hometown?"
>
> I shook my head for a long time in silence.
>
> The Muslim cried out from the mosque, and the rain sounded outside.
>
> You have remained with us for so long, you have become one of us.[22]

Kevin Carroll and Nigerian Art

The greater part of this account of the Oye-Ekiti scheme and its legacy of Africanizing Christian art in Nigeria focuses on the origins of the Oye-Ekiti Workshop and its art. Almost incidental to the Yoruba-Christian art fusion, Fathers Carroll, Kelly, and O'Mahony also developed a second and closely related art form in collaboration with important Yoruba artists. Currently referenced as Yoruba Neo-Traditional sculpture, this second workshop genre later received substantial critical attention from Yoruba specialists John Picton and Patrick Day of the School of Oriental and African Studies at the University of London.[1] While Carroll is recognized for collaborating on developing two small, but significant contemporary art genres, working with dozens of local artists in Yorubaland and the Middle Belt, and producing many hundreds of art pieces over almost five decades, his accomplishments on the broader scene of Nigerian contemporary art require consideration.

Reaction and Books

The Oye-Ekiti Workshop and its later decentralized art production stirred considerable attention, praise, criticism, and even opposition from unexpected sources. While Carroll certainly expected some colonial and Eurocentric reaction and opposition to these radical creations, opposition from local Yoruba Catholics who preferred the earlier European religious art then widespread in missionary Africa must have been a surprise to him and the others. Opposition to the Workshop within the Society of African Missions probably was not unexpected, but its vehemence was only a minor factor in securing Kelly's removal from office and probably was not foreseeable.[2] Interestingly, the negative reaction within the Nigerian Catholic community did not similarly apply to use of the Yoruba language, music, or textile embroidery in liturgical settings. These forms of cultural expression continue to flourish throughout Yorubaland, where they are tied to an evolving modern Yoruba identity, whereas the sculptural traditions outside of Ekiti had became obsolete or, in many urban contexts, such as Lagos, were entirely unknown.

In contrast, British colonial officials, especially scholarly cultural personnel and researchers, were preparing for African independence and welcomed the innovative Christian art development. Unexpected, too, must have been the sniping from a few expatriate or local modernist art spokespersons associated with universities or other competitive art projects, who were opposed to accepting the experimental Yoruba-Christian genre as an aspect of Nigerian visual modernity, creating a veritable cross fire within the emerging discourse of contemporary Nigerian art.

In 1967, a dozen years after he had left the workshop, Carroll finalized his manuscript for *Yoruba Religious Carving, Pagan & Christian Sculpture in Nigeria and Dahomey*, an important contribution to the scholarly study of Yoruba art as well as a more extensive introduction to the Oye-Ekiti experiment and its Yoruba-Christian genre. No longer content to spar with critics in small local journals, Carroll sought out major British and U.S. publishers (the Chapman and Praeger firms) that would be able to bring out a major pictorial and textual work during this early period in the development of Yoruba art studies. In his introductory comments, British author, scholar, and African art expert William Fagg describes Carroll's book as "one of the finest and most penetrating studies in the field."[3]

In this work, a product of his twenty years of on-site observation in Yorubaland, Carroll reviews the distant timeline for antecedents of modern Yoruba art, categorizes types of objects carved, discusses Yoruba religion and its practice, and analyzes the relationship of the art and religion, a masked festival, and the subject matter of this art as deeply representative of Yoruba life. Four major carvers—Areogun, Bandele, Lamidi, and Otooro—are profiled in the book, and the chapter on Areogun represents a rare record of one of the greatest twentieth-century Yoruba carving masters. The chapter on Bandele includes an equally invaluable account of a traditional Yoruba carver's description and analysis of his artistic process, a glossary of local terminology, and photographs of various stages of carving. The book became mandatory reading for a generation of Africanist art historians from the late 1960s into the 1980s.[4] More than two decades later, after his Middle Belt years, Carroll adapted his broad architectural research, earlier articles, and recent experiences in building the Gufanti and Papiri chapels into his *Architectures of Nigeria*, which focuses on traditional buildings as well as later developments in the western half of Nigeria.[5]

The Art Critics

In his 1967 book, Carroll writes that the Christian "work of the traditional carvers—cut in hard wood and so a permanent record of the struggle of the old Africa to turn to new ways—will increase in historical value as centuries pass. . . . Nevertheless the future of a deep Christian art lies not so much in their hands, as in those of the sophisticated [C]hristian artists of contemporary Africa."[6] His enthusiasm for the new art amplified his active, cooperative vision to include more artists—of more varied backgrounds and ethnicities—than the ones of the workshop era. For the next four decades of his life, Carroll continued to work with or sponsor any artist who was ready to cooperate in "the process of transforming the material culture of Catholic Christianity so that it represented the best of contemporary visual culture."[7]

In assessing this aspect of Kevin Carroll's contributions to Nigerian art, I found significant support and resources among people who knew him in an art-oriented capacity. Carroll's creative and collaborative work at Oye gained him both support and criticism in the wider Nigerian and British context.[8] An early observer associated with the British Museum, where he became Keeper of Ethnography, was anthropologist William Fagg, one of the great pioneers of African art studies in Britain; in the 1950s, he made extensive trips to Nigeria, where he became acquainted with Carroll and the Yoruba-Christian art project. Originally interested in the historic sculpture of Nigeria and author of several art and archaeology titles, Fagg came to rely on Carroll as a resource on the Ekiti carvers of the earlier period, including Areogun. He heaped praise on the workshop's Christian art project in his foreword to Carroll's *Yoruba Religious Carving*, describing it as an "enlightened experiment" that offered the serious prospect of reinvigorating Yoruba traditional sculpture. Not only had it demonstrated the "viability of Christianized traditional art," he observed, but it was also "harnessing contemporary art to the same purpose."⁹

Another acquaintance and supporter was British African art scholar Frank Willett, also Catholic, who wrote on the art and archaeology of Ile-Ife. A skilled observer of the contemporary art scene as well, Willett authored and revised over three decades his thematic *African Art* (1971) for a popular Thames and Hudson series and even included three pictures of Yoruba-Christian art carvings by Bandele, Lamidi, and Paul Osifo.¹⁰ Often used as a textbook, Willett's book was the first to include modernist African artwork.

The archive of Carroll's correspondence contains ample evidence of his value as a unique resource sought out by many of the early bright lights of the field, including Americans Roy Sieber, Robert Farris Thompson, and Henry John Drewal, who were doing research in the growing field of Yoruba art history. Combined with his fluency in Yoruba, Carroll's on-site interests and expertise in anything and everything in the visual arts proved a rich resource for many academics whose time in the field was limited, far short of Carroll's decades. Picton credits Carroll with mentoring him in Nigerian fieldwork when he was a newly arrived anthropologist in the early 1960s. He further commented that while other scholars often focused on the past, Carroll believed that the Catholic population wanted to be modern, "to participate in the evolution of a local modernity that drew upon the past when it was useful, but not to be constrained by it . . . and he made me take a serious interest in modernist developments, of which Catholic Christianity should be a lively part."¹¹

The Debate with Ulli Beier

Besides receiving ample praise from scholarly British Africanists, the new Yoruba-Christian genre drew criticism from an articulate and well-informed source: Ulli Beier (1922–2011), another expatriate arts commentator and author of a series of Yoruba and African art articles and books beginning in the 1950s. A young, secular, Jewish German refugee from Nazism to pre-war Palestine, Beier later took a degree in phonetics at the University of London, and this literary and visual arts enthusiast became an English literature instructor at University College Ibadan in 1950. In colonial Nigeria, he actively involved himself in creating extension courses in Yoruba history and culture in the years leading up to Nigerian independence.

Carroll and Beier encountered each other when Beier's new journal at

the University of Ife, *Odu: Journal of Yoruba Studies*, one of the major earlier resources for Nigerian arts, published Carroll's articles on local art as
early as 1955. In 1960, Beier opened a long-running debate over the value of
the Yoruba-Christian fusion in a small volume, *Art in Nigeria 1960*. In the
chapter "Beginnings of a Christian Art in Nigeria," he initially granted that
Oye-Ekiti was an "important artistic" development and a "bold and daring
experiment."[12] Then he posed what he found to be an insoluble dilemma:
"How then is it possible for an art-form that was inspired by traditional
Yoruba religion to be adapted to express Christian ideas?"[13] This tautological
question implied that such an adaptation could not succeed, that Yoruba art
techniques and style could serve only the purposes of traditional religion. Yet
Beier had earlier acknowledged: "The carver is regarded by the community as
a craftsman" and "does not even have to be a member of the cult for which he
carves."[14] Beier goes on to say that the new art form had "naïve charm and a
strong sense of the decorative" but opines in a caption that it is also "lacking
in power and concentration, basic characteristics of traditional Yoruba art."[15]
His conclusion seemed to be that "The Church has been able to provide the
carver with new work, but not with new inspiration . . . their figures are dull
and puppet-like"[16]

Eight years later, in his *Contemporary Art in Africa*, Beier repeats the
judgment in a gratuitously testy comment about the workshop's carvers, writing that "Were he a good Muslim, [Lamidi] would not carve at all" and that
Lamidi's colleague, George Bandele, "is only carving because he is not a very
orthodox Christian."[17] Further, he adds that the Neo-Traditional style of carving that Lamidi later developed for a new middle-class clientele in Ibadan was
becoming "increasingly dull and repetitive due to the commercialization of
his art."[18] And, finally, he suggests that since the carver's work had given way
to "empty fossilized forms," Lamidi had not "quite made the transition from
traditional carver to modern artist."[19] Beier skews his judgment by comparing
the fully developed carving tradition of an older generation of acknowledged
Opin-Ekiti masters such as Areogun and Bamgboye with relatively young
carvers working in Oye-Ekiti's two experimental modes.

Beier acknowledged in a 2008 communication that he had known but
one "good missionary," a fellow German who had "helped people out during
the Biafran war (1967–70)." This blanket statement covered missionaries not
just in Nigeria but also in Papua New Guinea, where Beier, ever the romantic
existentialist, had lived since 1968. He explained recently in a New Age tone
that "The *orisha* had also left Nigeria."[20]

Viewing Yoruba sculpture as a descriptive art form, Carroll gave a down-to-earth, cool, and analytical reply to Beier's oft-repeated criticisms. Focusing on Beier's basic assertion—that the traditional art was inseparable from the religion—he insisted that the content of Yoruba carving was not necessarily bound up in religious expression but was more humanistic in its subject matter. Carroll found it "hard to fully accept Ulli Beier's thesis that the traditional art is 'deeply expressive' of the pagan religion. There may be exceptions but I cannot find that intense expression of religious feeling in the work of the *Ekiti* or *Ketu* school of carvers, and I doubt that it exists in the work of other areas of Yoruba country."[21] Ever the exacting perfectionist, the modest yet realistic Carroll added that he saw "no reason why he should not continue to employ the traditional carvers on work suited to their limitations—though it is from the sophisticated and Christian artists, trained in modern art schools, that I chiefly hope for the development of deeply Christian art."[22]

Nevertheless, referring to the impact of early modernist artists Ben Enwonwu and Uche Okeke, John Picton suggests that the "broad sweep of Nigerian modernism was shaped by men who were Catholic, and while this had nothing to do with Carroll, he did have the wisdom to pick up on this."[23] By 1970, there were at least three modernist traditions in Nigerian art: first, Lamidi and the Neo-Traditional artists, including those who worked in the Yoruba-Christian mode; second, university fine art graduates; and, third, those who came out of the Oshogbo school, associated with internationally influential expatriates Suzanne Wenger and Ulli Beier.

It should be pointed out that the sting of Beier's influential comments abated somewhat in the case of Lamidi Fakeye when the internationally acclaimed carver was appointed to the art department of Obafemi Awolowo University in Ife in 1978, a position he held for more than two decades.[24] In fairness to the art world, as Carroll observed above, the Nigerian Catholic Church itself has only reluctantly and tardily tried to cultivate the cultural and artistic insights that both Kelly and Cardinal Costantini believed were crucial to the successful inculturation of Christianity, a process modeled extensively by Carroll and O'Mahony but infrequently by others.

As I pursued various strands of this mid-twentieth-century debate, John Picton, who had spent ten years in the 1960s and 1970s working on African art and archaeological research in southern Nigeria, was a remarkable source of insight. As a new arrival then, and associated with the Nigerian museum system, by 1960, Picton had already learned of Carroll's reputation among local and visiting British personnel and expatriates from William Fagg. As he developed a deep interest in Nigerian contemporary art, Picton spent time with Carroll, who provided the young London scholar with orientation and invaluable mentoring in the developing field of Nigerian art and culture, especially Yoruba topics. A long-term friendship ensued, with both men also sharing an interest in ongoing Christian inculturation issues, with which the Nigerian Catholic Church continued to engage, especially after the Second Vatican Council (1962–65) officially endorsed Costantini's inculturation policy.

Writing in 2002, Picton described Bandele as an accomplished artist displaying sculptural self-confidence and Lamidi as his most significant apprentice, and he critically summarized Carroll's attitude as believing that "what mattered was the skill of the artist, not the quality of his religious devotion."[25] The art scholar also recognized the by-product of the workshop, the Yoruba non-Christian traditional carvings done by Bandele, Lamidi, and their apprentices and relatives in and around Ibadan, acknowledging them as Yoruba Neo-Traditional sculpture and including the Yoruba-Christian genre as a subdivision.[26] In her 1997 review of "Lamidi Olonade Fakeye, a Retrospective Exhibition," held at Hope College, in Holland, Michigan, art historian Judith Perani commented that Lamidi's work had not received the same attention as that of some of his Ekiti predecessors because "the majority of his patrons have been regarded as nontraditional or inauthentic." She believed such views to be dated and noted that Fakeye's vision and voice "were clearly an important force in late twentieth century Yoruba art."[27]

Significantly, the Christian art genre developed in the Oye-Ekiti Workshop represented the first institutional program of inculturating Christian visual expression into a West African culture in modern times. It was also a highly visible step in the decolonization of the Catholic Church and its art in Nigeria. Both this Christian genre and its closely related genre of Yoruba Neo-Traditional carving were significant elements in the construction of cultural autonomy and the reassertion of nationalism and ethnicity through the continuities of traditional Yoruba visual culture before and during Nigerian liberation and independence. Carroll's decades of work and leadership in collaborating, commissioning, and writing about so many art projects for almost half a century deserve significant recognition.

Legacy of Yoruba-Christian Art

Carroll's religious community, the Irish Province of the Society of African Missions, increasingly recognized the significance of the Yoruba-Christian project, although earlier it had been divided on the program's goals, significance, and utility. In the years following Carroll's death in 1993, the province tried to secure his extant artwork still in its possession and to amass written and photographic records associated with the priest's ministry, which prominently featured his artistic inculturation activities. By 2001, the province had established an archive so that these printed resources would be available to interested scholars at its headquarters in Cork, Ireland (see Appendix). The province also accumulated Yoruba artwork, both Christian and traditional, associated with Carroll's long art patronage and mentoring career in its former seminary, Dromantine, a nineteenth-century manor house in rural County Down, Northern Ireland. By 2010, a small art gallery, the African Link, had been established there to showcase the largest collection of Kevin Carroll's art for visitors to Dromantine's conference center (see fig. 48).

Researching Yoruba-Christian Art

During my Nigerian field research in 2003 and 2006, an important participant and source, renowned sculptor Lamidi Fakeye, supplied me with information, contacts, and guidance that other sources could not have provided. Working with Lamidi gave me access to other crucial participants in the workshop project. Among these was Ajao Adetoye, son of Carroll's prime

Fig. 48. Dromantine Conference Centre, now the home of the Kevin Carroll Art Collection in the African Link Gallery, is the former seminary of the Irish Province of the SMA. Dromantine comprises an 1820s Georgian-style manor house and a number of acres in rural County Down, Northern Ireland. (NJB)

beadworker, Jimoh Adetoye, and childhood resident of the workshop (see fig. 50). The esteemed international carver also convened an informal reunion of workshop artists in the town of Oye-Ekiti. This meeting expanded my understanding of key art projects, notably the contributions of the women's head weaver, Christiana Comfort Ojo, and her husband, Joseph Ojo, age eighty-two and eighty-six respectively in 2006 (see fig. 51). Joseph, a music teacher and ethnomusicologist, described his lifelong collaboration with Carroll in adapting Christian hymns to local Yoruba linguistic and musical forms. Christiana provided a personal perspective that was completely missing from the workshop's records, that of a woman who had both sewn the outfits for the Three Kings in the Nativity sets for the 1950 "Exhibition of Sacred Art from the Missionlands" and been a key designer of workshop textiles. While in the Inisha area, a visit with Joseph Agbana, one of Carroll's primary carvers in his later years, provided an update on recent Yoruba-Christian commissions (see fig. 55). The SMA has preferred to use Joseph's skill in handling projects done in a Kevin Carroll fashion, such as the carving of doors and other important furnishings of the SMA House of Studies

Fig. 49 *(left)*. Lamidi Fakeye, age eighty-one, carving at his home studio in Ife, Nigeria, 2006. (NJB)

Fig. 50 *(right)*. Bead artist Ajao Adetoye, son of Jimoh Adetoye, the workshop's beadworker, displaying his own chiefly beadwork. (NJB)

Chapel in Bodija, Ibadan, where a plaque commemorates Kevin Carroll's work.

In Europe, initial surveys suggested that figures from the workshop's two exhibition Nativity sets (see ch. 4) had disappeared from both sight and the written record soon after the Rome exhibition went on tour to Madrid and Lisbon (1951–52). Afterward, these pieces reportedly were housed in the Vatican's Lateran Palace and Museum. Unfortunately, the records of the Vatican's Museum of Ethnology and Missiology (the institutional successor to the Lateran Museum, which closed in 1970) are silent on any pieces from the 1950 exhibition, much less on the Nativity set and other pieces from Oye-Ekiti, even though they had been published in brochures associated with their Iberian tour.[1]

On my early 2006 research visit to the library of Propaganda Fide's missionary university, the Urbaniana in Vatican City, an observant senior librarian was prompted by a color photo of the very similar Nativity #3 Yoruba-style Three Kings to locate and identify the Three Kings from Nativity #2, then serving as colorful but completely anonymous decor in the obscurity

Fig. 51. Lamidi Fakeye and the author visited surviving workshop participants in Oye-Ekiti in 2006, almost sixty years after the workshop was established. Head female weaver Christiana Comfort Ojo and her husband, Yoruba-Christian ethnomusicologist Joseph Ojo, describe their contributions to the workshop's program during most of its active years. (NJB)

of a university parlor (see fig. 20). Unfortunately, no other figures from the workshop's Rome exhibition collection, even, notably, the Holy Family figures, have been located. In a similar circumstance, the complete Nativity #3 as well as other workshop carvings from the period, made for Cardinal Costantini's special order in 1951, were located and identified at the small contemporary museum of the Italian lay Catholic organization Pro Civitate Christiana, in Assisi, earlier on the same Italian research visit (see fig. 2).

Later in 2006, I had another instructive and telling field experience on a research visit to St. Paul's Church, Ebute Metta, in Lagos, Nigeria (see ch. 5), but with a far different result. This church, built fifty years earlier, had been intended as a cosmopolitan showcase for the new Nigerian Christian art in the post-workshop Independence period. By this later date, however, it was clear that Carroll had been overly optimistic in his hopeful forecast that, with time, local discomfort with the church's innovative Africanized Christian art would diminish significantly. The church's exterior still included a huge, Hausa mud wall–style, dark and light pattern painted on its plaster facade (see fig. 35).[2]

Inside, Bandele's large Nativity figures (almost four feet tall) and his carved baptismal font, as well as Otooro's baptismal screen, had been pushed out of the way behind the altar; they were covered with dust and seemed of little ongoing usefulness. High on the side walls, Bruce Onobrakpeya's large, painted Stations of the Cross seemed similarly dusty, with paint flaking off, and was insecurely fastened to the wall. Even more obvious marginalization and utter neglect completed the interior experience: Benin sculptor Paul Osagie Osifo's imposing African Madonna carving, still wall-mounted in her prominent side altar niche, was now layered with dust and hidden behind

Fig. 52 (A and B). Joseph Agbana, one of Father Carroll's most reliable carvers in the later decades, and his son continue to carve in both the Yoruba-Christian and the Neo-Traditional styles in their studio in Inisha. (NJB)

a statue of Our Lady of Fatima, a popular European devotional Mary image (see fig. 53). The situation ironically recalled Carroll's caution against alternative titles and secondary devotions, such as Fatima, Lourdes, or Guadalupe, which, in newly Christian countries, obscure Mary's "first and chief title" as mother of Christ, "her most essential theme."[3] As an art patron, Carroll had always stressed biblical and liturgical themes over competing trends in devotional art.

Outside, there was a final and deliberately violent message on the church's imposing double front doors. Likely the largest and most impressive work of Yoruba-Christian art, these great doors feature ten of Lamidi's Yoruba-Christian panels, dramatically carved through front to back, making them an imposing yet particularly fragile masterpiece. One's eyes are quickly drawn to a lower central panel of the Yoruba Transfiguration, which celebrates Yoruba traditional religion as a worthy precursor to the Christian message. Here, in this panel spotlighting Carroll's farsighted and generous Christian artistic statement, is the figure of a beheaded priest of Shango, standing on the right side of the Risen Christ (see fig. 54). This headless representative of the rarely depicted *orisha* Shango—one of the most popular traditional *orisha*, who here parallels Moses (and the Law) in the Gospel's Transfiguration passage—appears as the victim of a deliberate act of lethal iconoclasm.

A follow-up interview with internationally recognized artist Bruce Onobrakpeya led to a flood of comments about Carroll's positive influence on his career and on mid-twentieth-century Nigerian art in general (see

Fig. 53 *(top)*. Paul Osagie Osifo's wall-mounted African Madonna, St. Paul's Church, in the Lagos suburb of Ebute Metta, 2006. Although placed in a prominent side altar originally, the Madonna is currently blocked from view by a European Marian image. (NJB)

Fig. 54 *(bottom)*. A panel of Lamidi Fakeye's massive carved-through double doors, St. Paul's Church. The panel celebrates the Yoruba Transfiguration, Father Carroll's brave statement of Christian respect for the indigenous local religion. Here, the figure of a priest of Shango standing on the right side of the Risen Christ had been beheaded. (NJB)

Fig. 55. Multimedia artist Bruce Onobrakpeya in his three-story art studio, Ovuomauro, located in the Mushin suburb of Lagos. Onobrakpeya attributes his career as a successful, internationally honored arts figure to Father Carroll's early patronage, which began in 1967 when the artist created his massive Stations of the Cross for St. Paul's Church. (NJB)

fig. 55). Hearing of the sad condition of not only his Stations paintings but also much of the original art installations from the 1960s, the widely honored contemporary artist announced his intention to go over to the church immediately and put at least his paintings right. Onobrakpeya, a painter, printmaker, and sculptor, applauded Carroll as a highly significant force in the emergence of contemporary artists during Nigeria's nascent Independence period and credited Carroll with providing and securing crucial commissions for him, when he was young and as yet unrecognized, and others.[4]

Carroll's Legacy and an Exhibition

Investigating the location and condition of the Oye-Ekiti Workshop's legacy more than a decade after Carroll's death revealed the struggle for survival of this praised, criticized, ignored, and defaced genre in the possession of reluctant, unenthusiastic, or inattentive religious institutions. This dramatically expanded view of extant works of Yoruba-Christian art in the Oye-Ekiti tradition increased the material basis for a fully documented and representative exhibition of Oye-Ekiti's Christian art fusion in the near future. The exhibition is being organized under the auspices of the SMA's Dromantine Conference Centre in Northern Ireland and the African Art Museum of the

SMA Fathers in Tenafly, New Jersey, near New York City. This presentation draws on the findings from three continents and addresses an equally global audience with its message of cultural understanding, belief and hope, and resistance to cultural domination.

Clearly, Africanized Christian art still provokes response and reaction, as it did in the 1950s when, for some, it symbolized resistance to colonialism and Eurocentric values and attitudes as graphically demonstrated in St. Paul's Church. Churches that contain unprotected, though significant artistic embellishments and furnishings face the increasing threat of both vandalism and theft, in addition to the effects of weather and normal use. Eventually, with greater awareness of the significance of artworks that are regularly subjected to extensive public exposure (especially the rare and valuable carved doors of St. Paul's or other imagery from the workshop), the Church and other institutional authorities should increase their attention to preserving, protecting, and raising educational awareness of such pieces. Necessarily, local church security, custodial, and maintenance issues need to be effectively addressed, not just by the Lagos Archdiocese and its clergy but by other pastors and dioceses. All need to be alerted to the presence of these significant expressions of the Independence era and of the Nigerian Catholic Church's own decolonization-inculturation era, when a colonial "missionland" was replaced by a national Catholic Church.

Currently, the workshop's art, undeniably a valuable part of both the Catholic Church's religious heritage and Nigeria's national patrimony, still provides an imaginative, indigenous alternative to the conventional, predictable, and ubiquitous religious imagery of Euro-Christianity. For Yoruba and other Nigerians, the genre also continues to invite and challenge viewers, regardless of religious or ethnic heritage (including their historic and contemporary belief systems), as worthy and memorable legacies. Recognition of the Yoruba-Christian genre extends beyond Africa, as Christianity, including its largest component, Roman Catholicism, becomes more of a truly global religion, displaying explosive growth in Africa, Asia, and Latin America and heralding the global drift of the bulk of Christianity toward the Southern Hemisphere in the third millennium of the Common Era.

Areas of Further Research

Reflecting on a decade of research on this Yoruba-Christian art experiment, some notable areas of further investigation seem clear. The limited acceptance of the genre within various groups and levels of a Catholic community that is divided on the issue of inculturation and the highly mixed circumstances of the artworks' fate in the hands of non-African institutions provide rich grounds for further specialized research. A deeper analysis of the workshop's closure in 1954, especially the cultural, pastoral, theological, and financial elements, also await an interested investigator.

Useful as well would be a definitive inventory of the genre, something Picton has long suggested and I have only partially completed. As part of this effort, I am circulating photos of the missing Nativity painting and pieces mentioned in chapter 4, drawn from the Carroll archive photo collection. Additional subjects for further exploration are the nature of the relationship between the mentors and the artists and the scale of the workshop, which was inevitably diminished by financial, cultural, pastoral, and theological obstacles, and its isolation, as almost the only experiment in a localized genre of African Christian art in West Africa. Other important products of Carroll's broader Nigerian patronage await focused art historical research, most notably, Bruce Onobrakpeya's fourteen Stations of the Cross. In fact, the entire site of St. Paul's in Ebute Metta presents a meaningful example of the disjunction between Catholic art theory and popular perception. An equally intriguing, though seemingly nebulous, subject is the widespread reluctance of Euroamerican scholars to engage professionally with Christian art in both the twentieth and twenty-first centuries.

For an Irish SMA pastor in Ibadan, who succinctly, but glumly, summarized the project—"It was too little, too late"—the genre did not seem to catch fire. Yet Kelly's goal of an indigenized Christian art was smartly achieved in the hands of Carroll, O'Mahony, and various artists over the course of four decades. Still, this was but a single brief experiment with a definite and somewhat limited impact. The breakup of the workshop setting in 1954 also removed some momentum and synergy among patrons and artists, making creative collaboration slower and difficult. The continuation of Christian art patronage by both Carroll and O'Mahony under these decentralized circumstances reduced the workshop's production and its public relations impact. At the same time, the closure thrust Carroll's perspective and patronage onto the national stage. Earlier, many Church figures, local Yoruba clergy, and Irish bishops in Nigerian dioceses, as well as members of the SMA's Irish Province, had reservations about this unusual Africanized Christian art.[5] Despite the public and published promotion of this art form in books and international exhibitions sponsored by Celso Costantini and

Propaganda Fide, the early influence of racist, colonial, and unconvinced missionary attitudes lingered.[6]

Kelly's hope that this new indigenous art form could be developed by local artists as yet "untainted" by exposure to European imagery and values, based on Costantini's admonition to avoid "Europeanism" and "foreign feeling," was unrealistic in colonial Yorubaland of the 1940s. European visuality, both religious and commercial, was ubiquitous in mid-twentieth-century Nigeria. This is evident even in the very *Nigeria Magazine* of 1950 in which Carroll's introductory article on the Yoruba-Christian experiment appeared (see ch. 4). The article's text is accompanied by numerous examples of British advertising imagery clearly directed at an educated Nigerian clientele and promoting a variety of colonial consumer products. That European imagery had already taken deep root in the Nigerian visual culture. This can be seen from Lamidi's and Carroll's separate accounts of their first meeting, when the young, marginally trained Lamidi Fakeye approached Kevin Carroll for work at the Oye-Ekiti Workshop and carved a European-style angel, believing this to be the sort of religious figure that Carroll would want. Lamidi, a young convert to Islam from rural Ekiti, had already been familiarized with European Christian art, likely through his attendance at a missionary-run secondary school.

As Picton has observed, Kevin Carroll was a modernizer and did not share Kelly's desire to restore Yoruba culture to some kind of traditional purity. His conceptions developed and changed as his relationships with the artists and carvers deepened. Having observed earlier that the Oye craftspeople he encountered were rarely Catholic, he prized Bandele's awareness of the Catholic religion, traditionally trained hand and eye, and lineage of artistic descent from Areogun and other great Opin-Ekiti carvers. Through his work with Bandele, Carroll came to appreciate the potential that Lamidi represented by his higher level of formal education as well as his family's five generations of professional carving. In the following years, the workshop's developing skill and familiarity with the Yoruba religion and its visual expression certainly took on more prominence than any issue of religious affiliation, as is seen in Carroll's eagerness to have Areogun work on Yoruba-Christian subject matter despite the eminent carver's lifelong adherence to his ancestral religion.

During the life of the Oye-Ekiti Workshop, opposition to the workshop grew stronger within the SMA and among other Catholic clergy and the

Nigerian hierarchy. The once standard hostility to the indigenous religion among European missionaries could not be reversed quickly. The missionaries tended to be lukewarm or indifferent, viewing the workshop as experimental and of unproved benefit in comparison to work such as the formation of catechists and the establishment of outstations, schools, clinics, and churches. During the workshop's lifetime, the creation of self-supporting missions was a top priority within the SMA and its missions, so opposition was based primarily on the cost of the scheme. After this radical art experiment moved with Carroll from rural Ekiti to a more urban setting, such as St. Paul's in Lagos in the late 1950s, much of the opposition came from resident lay parishioners who had long been exposed to European Christian imagery. Some among the Lagos Catholic population were descended from emancipated slaves, repatriated from Brazil and Cuba in the nineteenth century. In 1863, Francesco Borghero, SMA, was the first Catholic missionary priest to the region that would later become Nigeria. When he arrived in Lagos, twelve hundred people who already identified themselves as Catholics reportedly greeted him.[7] It was hardly likely that such urban groups would be easily won over to the startlingly different style of an indigenized Christian art fusion like that of the Oye-Ekiti Workshop and its Opin-Ekiti style of sculpture.

Carroll's records in the SMA Irish archive are replete with evidence of support for the art project from both British colonial officials and European and American scholars. Orders for art pieces came from interested Catholics across Europe and North America. The idea of an indigenous Christian art strongly appealed to Catholics and other Christians in the era of African independence from colonial rule and the civil rights struggle in the United States. From the ongoing dispute about the merits of Christian-African art within St. Paul's parish, Bruce Onobrakpeya quoted a negative voice, writing to the effect that the usual proponents of Africanized church art often seemed to be European priests who were "trying, by hook or crook, to force" African art "into the liturgy of the Church in Africa."[8]

From the start, Kelly's transformational art project needed an accompanying advertising and reeducation program for both the local people and the members of his own missionary clergy. The inculturation approach favored and promoted by Cardinal Costantini during his twenty-year tenure as head of Propaganda Fide had won limited support, and the Oye-Ekiti Workshop was one of very few attempts to put his ideas into practice. The other attempts were scattered and on a smaller scale. The influence, example, and impact of Costantini's ideas and leadership could not easily overcome decades of embedded colonial-era racism and Eurocentric attitudes within the clergy and hierarchy.

Only with the dawning of political independence in Africa and the opportunity for Christian renewal through a universal Church Council (Vatican II, 1962–65) did these experiments attract serious attention and belatedly win the argument about respecting indigenous peoples and their cultures. Nevertheless, during the harsh colonial transition to Nigerian and African modernity, profoundly original thought, genuine goodwill, and sincerely motivated creativity combined with customary local ideals of spiritual power and beauty to produce this unique Yoruba-Christian genre. Indigenized African Christian art clearly demonstrates that Christian conversion could be a less culturally destructive experience, precluding the necessity of becoming European in order to become Christian. In our post-colonial, postmodern, and global era, the brave examples provided by the early innovators mentioned in this book can be inspirational for a new generation of Christian advocates who must face new and different challenges in the third millennium. For non-Christians, Yoruba-Christian art, besides being an example of resistance to externally imposed cultural domination and indoctrination, is also a model of a more respectful, imaginative, and humane alternative in cross-cultural visual communication between groups with unequal resources and historical advantages.

Comparing the contemporary world with the era discussed here, it is clear that the twenty-first century presents very different circumstances from those faced by Costantini, Kelly, and Carroll half a century ago. Their examples nevertheless offer important understandings, even lessons, for religious, artists, Christians, and other interested observers. From his vantage point, serving first as a Vatican diplomat in China and then as a senior administrator in Propaganda Fide, Celso Costantini accurately perceived the destructive forces of European and Japanese imperialism. Together with Pius XI, he accelerated what up to then had been a sluggish decolonization of the Church, revising its relationship and identification with expansionist powers. He also initiated a process of decentralization, moving what had been a profoundly Eurocentric Church, culturally, liturgically, and theologically, toward a more global perspective. Costantini shared with SMA founder Bishop Brésillac two related goals for the Church beyond Europe: the creation, consolidation, and expansion of an indigenous clergy and the promotion of wider cultural awareness and, ultimately, cultural pluralism, notably in religious art.

Doubtless unaware of the long-term influence they would exercise, Costantini, Brésillac, and their followers were significant and influential participants in the southward shift of Catholicism and, indeed, the movement of Christianity toward a non-European, non-white–majority Christian demographic. This great religious shift, currently under way, has reversed deep Eurocentric social and cultural patterns of the past centuries. Kelly's Oye-Ekiti scheme was an early, but significant, indicator of this fundamental change in Christianity's center of gravity. For Yoruba and other Nigerians, the genre continues to invite and challenge viewers, regardless of religious or ethnic heritage, as worthwhile, memorable legacies, equal to any. And as Christianity, including Catholicism, continues to display dynamic growth in membership, especially in Africa, Asia, and Latin America, and becomes a truly global religion, the art of the Oye-Ekiti Workshop deserves recognition for epitomizing the blooming of the Christian message on Africa's soil and for heralding the global realignment of Christianity toward the Southern Hemisphere in the third millennium of the Common Era.

African Cultural Resources of the SMA

In France in the 1850s, Bishop Melchior de Marion Brésillac (1813–1859) founded a missionary group destined for West Africa, the Society of African Missions. He imbued it with a strong priority not only to evangelize local peoples but also form a local clergy to replace European missionaries and make the mission self-governing and self-sufficient. Implicit in this drive was the necessity of understanding the local language and way of life. This basic orientation and sensitivity were sometimes strongly at odds with dominant racist, colonial, and Eurocentric attitudes throughout the nineteenth century.

The indigenization of the Church was a disputed issue. In India, some of the older religious orders did not feel that it was practicable or possible to envisage an Indian clergy or hierarchy. Younger societies, such as the Paris Foreign Missionary Society, to which Brésillac then belonged, took the opposite view. They believed indigenization could and should take place without delay. Before he became a bishop, Brésillac was in charge of a seminary where the students were all Indian. Propaganda Fide backed the younger missionary groups and strongly advocated the idea of forming an indigenous clergy and hierarchy. The practice of respecting and preserving the culture of the peoples served by SMA also became integral to Brésillac's vision. Consequently, over the intervening century and a half, the SMA has been at the forefront in fostering greater public awareness and appreciation of African cultures through an international system of cultural resources: museum centers of art and an archive of documentation in the Society's various provinces in Europe and the United States. The following are brief descriptions of these collections.

THE IRISH PROVINCE: THE KEVIN CARROLL COLLECTION (KCC)

Foremost among these resource centers for readers of this book are the archives of the Irish Province of the Society of African Missions, based at Blackrock Road, Cork, Ireland. This holding contains the Kevin Carroll Collection, created in 2001, comprising the writings, files, correspondence, and photographic work of Father Kevin Carroll.

THE ARCHIVE, CORK, IRELAND

Kevin Carroll's written records and publications, on file in the Archive of the Irish Province at the provincial headquarters in Cork, Ireland, are extensive and organized to provide assistance to scholars and researchers interested in his work and the people and cultures his written work addressed.

Unusual among the holdings is Carroll's extensive photographic record of the Oye-Ekiti artists and art production, which extends beyond the workshop years to the end of his career in 1993. Both documentary and photographic collections were essential to this book and multiple journal articles and conference papers in this field.

In addition to his major role as art patron in developing Yoruba-Christian art and supporting artists with commissions over the years, Carroll became known beyond Yorubaland as a keen observer of other local peoples and ways of life while he was stationed around the southwestern and Middle Belt areas of Nigeria from the mid-twentieth century onward. In his spare time and on his travels, Carroll observed local peoples and created an ethnographic record in his extensive collection of photographs (see APP figs. 1 and 2). He also mastered three indigenous languages besides Yoruba: Hausa, Kamberi, and Tiv.

Carroll's legacy preserved in Cork includes a collection of some four thousand photographs spanning his fifty years of missionary work in Africa and covers all aspects of life in Nigeria in a number of topic areas: religious, social, cultural, and artistic (see APP fig. 3). There is also extensive documentation related to his life's work, including information on the photographic collection, administrative and academic correspondence, diaries, and publications. Important, too, is a two-hour audio recording of an interview about his long career, made in 1992, shortly before his passing. Many of the

APP fig. 1 *(top)*. Father Carroll, 1964, taking photos during one of his frequent ethnographic field jaunts through Yorubaland and Nigeria. The three women dancers are being initiated into the rites of that temple by their "novice master" in green. (John Picton, reproduced by permission of the National Commission for Museums and Monuments, Nigeria)

APP fig. 2 *(bottom)*. Father Carroll pursuing fieldwork on the art and religious practices of the Ketu Yoruba in neighboring Dahomey (now Benin Republic). Carroll is photographing a boy who demonstrates how the mask and breastplate are worn in the open enclosure where *gelede* masks were then kept in a relatively inaccessible village of the Ohori-Ije people in 1964. (John Picton, reproduced by permission of the National Commission for Museums and Monuments, Nigeria)

APP fig. 3. Male dancer, photographed
by Carroll in Nigeria's rural Middle Belt,
is one of many in his ethnographic visual
documents in the Kevin Carroll Photo
Collection in Cork, Ireland. (KCC)

photographs have now been scanned to computer files and are available in
electronic form.

Although the archive is private, it welcomes and encourages scholars
who wish to consult the Kevin Carroll Collection. Information relating to
the archive may be found on the SMA Irish Province's website, www.sma.ie.

THE KEVIN CARROLL ART COLLECTION, DROMANTINE, COUNTY DOWN, NORTHERN IRELAND

This collection is housed in the African Link Gallery, which is part of the
SMA's Dromantine Conference Centre. It is the largest collection of Yoruba-
Christian Art outside of the church assemblages and installations in Nigeria.
Still under development, Dromantine's Kevin Carroll Art Collection in-
cludes unique Yoruba-Christian art pieces, among them, notably, Nativity
sets and Stations of the Cross by carver George Bandele. One exceptional
work by Bandele includes an exquisite altar bookstand (*thabor*) carved with
Gospel scenes (see APP fig. 4).

Reflecting the art production of the Oye-Ekiti Workshop and the two
SMA patrons, a number of important Yoruba traditional carvings include
divination pieces as well as Epa and Gelede masks by workshop artists Bandele, Fakeye, and Otooro are on display in the Conference Center's recently

APP fig. 4 *(top)*. Finely carved altar book stand by George Bandele Areogun, Oye-Ekiti, ca. 1950 from the Kevin Carroll Art Collection in Dromantine. (NJB)

APP fig. 5 *(bottom)*. Entry doors were recently carved by Joseph Agbana of Inisha for the Kevin Carroll Art Collection housed at Dromantine Conference Centre, County Down, Northern Ireland. (NJB)

completed African Link Gallery. A prominent recent addition is the Yoruba-Christian double doors by carver Joseph Agbana, installed in 2010 (see APP fig. 5).

THE AFRICAN ART MUSEUM OF THE SMA FATHERS, TENAFLY, NEW JERSEY, AMERICAN PROVINCE

The African Art Museum of the SMA Fathers, or SMA African Art Museum, is part of the mission complex built by the American Province of the SMA in 1963. Today, it is a public museum with collections of almost 2,000 African objects drawn from most of the art-producing areas of sub-Saharan Africa. The core of the Tenafly collections is composed of pieces contributed by American missionary priests returning from Africa or purchased from the European SMA museums or an occasional dealer. The bulk of material related to the Oye-Ekiti scheme and the activities of Father Kevin Carroll was acquired between 1968 and 1978, when Father Kevin Scanlan was provincial superior at Tenafly. At Scanlan's request, Father Carroll commissioned a number of pieces directly from Ekiti artists for the new museum in Tenafly. These include a set of four doors, a Crucifixion, and a Virgin Mary by George Bandele of Osi-Ilorun; a large Epa mask, probably made by Lamidi Fakeye when he was apprenticed to Bandele; a crèche set by Joseph Imale with beadwork by Jimoh Adetoye; and *The Stations of the Cross,* a set of fourteen prints by Bruce Onobrakpeya of Lagos.

A much later acquisition is one of the Three Kings of the Christian Nativity with Eshu characteristics, by Areogun, carved in 1953 and purchased from Father Sean O'Mahony of the Irish Province in 1999. A complete inventory of works related to Father Kevin Carroll is available on the museum's website, smausa@smafathers.org. In 2013, the SMA African Art Museum, working with the author as a guest curator, will host an exhibition drawn from collections of Yoruba-Christian works in the United States, Europe, and Africa.

The Tenafly collections have been shaped very carefully since 1980 by the museum's first curator, William Siegmann, and then by volunteer curator Charles Bordogna and dealer-scholar Leonard Kahan. Robert J. Koenig, director since 1996, has built very strong groups of objects from Liberia, Mali, Nigeria, and Burkina Faso on that foundation. Utilitarian and ceremonial terra-cottas, textiles, and costumes are all very well represented. The collection of Bamana *bogolan* and *bogolanfini* is among the best in the world. A mural-size Crucifixion, more than one hundred years old, which hangs in the

APP fig. 6. Carved panel from Bandele's doors in the African Art Museum of the SMA Fathers in Tenafly, N.J., showing a scene from the slave trade in Nigerian history.

St. Anthony Chapel adjacent to the museum galleries, is the highlight of a small but choice group of Ethiopian works. A monumental commemorative statue of Salif Keita, Mali's greatest soccer player, made by an anonymous Baule carver, stands eleven feet high in the museum rotunda. The museum organizes several exhibitions a year, drawing on objects from its permanent collections and on loan from public and private collections in the New York metropolitan area. These are always documented in checklists or catalogues. Among the more recent exhibitions are *Sogo Bo: The Animals Come Forth: Malian Puppets and Masks from the Rosen Collection* (2009); *The Discerning Eye: African Art from the Collection of Carl and Wilma Zabel* (2007); and *African Mud Cloth: The Bogolanfini Art Tradition of Gneli Traoré of Mali* (2006). Forthcoming is *Fifty Years of Collecting: An Illustrated Guide to the African Art Museum of the SMA Fathers* (2011), with a catalogue published with the support of the New Jersey State Council on the Arts and Department of State through funds distributed by the Bergen County Department of Parks, Division of Cultural Affairs. The museum has an educational program for students of all ages. The galleries are open seven days a week, 10 a.m. to 5 p.m., and admission is free.

The African Art Museum of the SMA Fathers, 23 Bliss Avenue, Tenafly, New Jersey, 07670. Tel. (201) 894-8611; fax (201) 541-1280; e-mail museum@ smafathers.org; website, http://www.smafathers.org/. President, Board of Trustees, Fr. Michael Moran, SMA; Director, Robert J. Koenig.

APP fig. 7. One of fourteen linocut prints of *The Stations of the Cross* by Bruce Onobrakpeya, at the African Art Museum of the SMA Fathers, Tenafly, N.J. (NJB)

OTHER SMA AFRICAN CULTURAL RESOURCES IN EUROPE

Afrika Centrum (Africa Center), Cadier-en-Keer (near Maastricht), Netherlands. Focuses on the art and daily life of Ghana. www.afrikacentrum.nl

Musée Africain des Cultures de l'Afrique de l'Ouest, Lyon, France. A well-developed African art museum with an emphasis on West Africa. www.musee-africain-lyon.org

NOTES

PREFACE

    1. Carroll 1967.

    2. John Picton, personal communication, March 30, 2009.

    3. Ostling 1989, 76–77.

INTRODUCTION

    1. Nicholas J. Bridger, *The Oye-Ekiti Workshop (1947–1954), a Study in Nigerian Colonial Patronage*, unpublished M.A. thesis, San Francisco State University, 2002. This original study establishes the documentary basis for much of the present account of the Oye-Ekiti Workshop.

    2. Kasfir 1999, 53.

    3. Clark 1998, 30.

    4. Barrett and Johnson 2004, 25.

    5. O'Brien and Palmer 2007, 23

    6. Falola 2008, 13

    7. Costantini 1940.

    8. Picton speculates that this scholarly neglect is due to "Western" intellectual embarrassment with Christianity, lingering misperception of twentieth-century developments in Africa, and divided opinion within Nigeria (like the Ulli Beier critique in ch. 6) and within the Church itself over the extent of inculturation (personal communication, May 17, 2011).

    9. Ostling 1989.

    10. Peel 2000, 1.

CHAPTER 1

    1. Walls 1996, 173.

    2. Ibid.

3. Ibid., in Latin, "Extra Ecclesiam Nulla Salus."

4. Ibid., xix.

5. Thornton 1984, 149.

6. Thornton 1992, 257.

7. Bailey 1999, 95–105.

8. Hogan 1990, 58.

9. Ibid., 59.

10. Kirby 1994, 59.

11. Ibid., 61.

12. Ekechukwu 1988, 137.

13. Lugira 1962, 130.

14. Early evidence of the shift was apparent in the Vatican's 1925 "Exhibition of Religious Art from the Missionlands"; see Costantini 1940, 19.

15. Ibid.

16. Ibid.

17. Celso Costantini published a first edition of *L'Arte Cristiana nelle Missioni, Manuale d'Arte Per I Missionari* in Rome in 1940; it was apparently published in at least three of the major colonial languages in Africa, Italian, French, and English. In 1949, a slightly expanded version was published, also in at least those three languages. The later French version is Celso Costantini, *L'Art Chrétien dans les Missions, Manuel d'Art pour les Missionaires*, translated by Edmond Leclef (Paris: Desclee, De Brouwer, 1949). The later volume appears to be an update of the earlier edition, with little change. The two editions seem to approximately coincide with the two dates of the "Exhibition of Sacred Art from the Missionlands," 1940 and 1950.

CHAPTER 2

1. Costantini 1940.

2. Kelly 1947.

3. Ibid., 33.

4. Ibid., 30.

5. Ibid.

6. Ibid.

7. Ibid., 60.

8. Ibid.

9. Ibid., 51.

10. Kelly 1947.

11. Kevin F. Carroll, SMA Obituary 1993, KCC.

12. Carroll 1982, 2.

13. Carroll 1967.

14. Carroll 1969, 13.

15. Carroll 1982, 2.

CHAPTER 3

1. Walker 1998, 13–15.

2. Picton 1994, 24.

3. Carroll 1967, 1.

4. Carroll 1969, 1.

5. Carroll 1967, 2–3.

6. Ibid., 1.

7. Ibid., 4–5.

8. Ibid., 3.

9. In his midcourse assessment of the workshop as Irish provincial and workshop instigator, in his unpublished "Confidential Notes" (KCC), 1950, n.p.

10. Kelly 1950.

11. Fakeye et al. 1996, 92.

12. Picton 2002, 100.

13. Carroll 1967, 91–93.

14. Picton 2002, 100.

15. Carroll 1967, 91.

16. Carroll 1978, 7.

17. Carroll 1967.

18. Ibid., 4.

19. Ibid.

20. Ibid.

21. Carroll 1967.

22. Picton 1994, 8.

23. Carroll 1967, 86.

24. Peel 2000, 263.

25. In 2003, I visited the rectory where Father Carroll died in 1993, St. Leo's parish in Ibadan, and placed the whereabouts and identification of one of Areogun's Three Kings; in 2007, during a visit to the African Art Museum of the SMA Fathers in Tenafly, New Jersey, I located and corrected the identification of a second King who was in the form of the *orisha* Eshu, acquired from Sean O'Mahony. The third King carving has not been located.

26. Carroll 1978, n.p.

27. Fakeye et al. 1996, 94–95.

28. Carroll 1959, 1.

29. Carroll 1967, 106.

30. Fakeye et al. 1996, 83.

31. Kasfir 1999, 96.

32. Carroll 1959, 2.

33. Carroll 1966.

34. Fakeye et al. 1996, 95.

35. Ibid., 96.

36. Ibid.

37. Ibid.
38. Fagg 1969, 52.
39. Ibid.

CHAPTER 4

1. Carroll 1950.
2. Bruzzichelli 1963, n.p.
3. Carroll, HW Notes, Color Album 3, KCC.
4. Personal communication from Rev. Patrick Carroll, SMA, Kevin Carroll's younger brother, August 6, 2008.
5. Carroll, HW Notes, Color Album 3, KCC.
6. John Pemberton, *Divination*, in Metmuseum.org.
7. Carroll 1950, 353.
8. Satolli 1952.
9. Bruzzichelli 1962, n.p.
10. Carroll 1967, 121.
11. Lamidi Fakeye, interview with author, 2003.
12. Carroll 1967, 153.
13. John Picton, personal communication, May 18, 2011.
14. Carroll 1967, 131.
15. Stanley 2003, 4, 7.
16. Peel 1989.
17. Stanley 2003, 4, 7.

CHAPTER 5

1. Carroll 1982.
2. Kelly 1950, 11.
3. Fakeye et al. 1996, 117–133.
4. Ibid., 115.
5. Carroll 1967, 132.
6. Ibid., 133.
7. Ibid.
8. Ibid.
9. Ibid., 134.
10. Ibid., 132–133.
11. Carroll 1981, 3–5.
12. Ibid., 3.
13. Ibid., 3.
14. Ibid., 5.
15. Carroll 1991.
16. Ibid.
17. Ibid.
18. Ibid.

19. John Picton, personal communication, 2006.

20. Carroll 1991.

21. Carroll 1981, 5.

22. Joseph Ojo's *oriki*, anonymous translation provided by SMA Archive, Cork, Ireland.

CHAPTER 6

1. See Picton 2002 and Day 1999. The "Neo-Traditional" label for such developments may have been popularized by Nigerian art historians. See Lawal 1977, 145–146; and Jegede 1984.

2. SMA archivist's note: "Kelly's removal was caused by serious problems in the home houses (Ireland). It had nothing to do with opposition to the Oye-Ekiti scheme. The scheme was regarded as somewhat of a curiosity within the province. Most people were indifferent. A small number were enthusiastic and an equally small number were vehemently opposed, although the grounds were rarely linked to an abhorrence of the idea of using African art for church purposes. Generally the scheme was supported by those in leadership roles until the cost of supporting it became a problem. The scheme was costing the Province a lot of money. It was felt that money could be better spent building churches, schools and clinics, rather than on a rarefied experimental project. When the scheme was closed—and money no longer was an issue—increasing numbers of the men (especially the younger) bought into the scheme's central insight and Carroll was increasingly in demand as an advisor on church furnishings and construction. The respect for his work is evident in the number of articles written by him which were published in the Society's Magazine—the *African Missionary*). The link between the Workshop Scheme and Kelly's removal was indirect. It was felt that as Provincial he should have paid more attention to the Home Houses and less to what was going on in Africa. He had failed to see serious trouble coming in the Home Houses, but it was this 'trouble', not the Scheme, which led to his removal."

3. Carroll 1967, ix.

4. In UC Berkeley's undergraduate reading library, I found almost two dozen heavily marked, worn, dog-eared copies of Carroll's 1967 book, clearly residue from earlier decades of reserve-shelf-reading requirements.

5. Carroll 1992.

6. Ibid., 133.

7. Picton, e-mail to author, 2009.

8. A series of British Africanist art scholars, by discipline either anthropologists or archaeologists, who coincidentally were also all Catholic, similarly viewed Carroll's contributions with much appreciation and understanding. They include William Fagg, and his brother, Bernard Fagg, Frank Willett, and John Picton. Bernard Fagg founded the National Museum in Jos (after locating the two-thousand-year-old Nok culture near there) and later became the curator of the Pitt Rivers Museum in Oxford in 1963. Others are mentioned in the text.

9. Carroll 1967, ix–x.

10. Willett 1971.

11. Picton, e-mail to author, 2009.

12. Beier 1960, 14–15.

13. Ibid., 14.

14. Beier 1957, 17

15. Beier 1957.

16. Quoted in Carroll 1967, 70.

17. Beier, 1960, plates 38, 39, 40.

18. Beier 1968, 25–26.

19. Ibid., 27.

20. Beier, e-mail to author, 2008.

21. Carroll 1967, 70.

22. Ibid., 72.

23. Picton, personal communication, May 17, 2011.

24. While Carroll did not respond to Beier's gratuitous and subjective criticism of Bandele and Lamidi, the artists still felt decades later that Beier's ad hominem comments had unfairly and inappropriately judged them and damaged the genre's acceptance in Nigerian and international art circles. Personal communication, Professor Moyo Okedigi, a colleague of Fakeye's at Obafemi Awolowo University, Ife, Nigeria, 2007.

25. Picton 2002, 100.

26. Ibid., 100–101.

27. Perani 1997, 81.

EPILOGUE

1. Satolli 1952.

2. Carroll, 1967, 126.

3. Ibid., 138.

4. Bruce Onobrakpeya, interview by author, August 2006.

5. A personal observation of the Irish SMA's archivist, Rev. Edmund Hogan, SMA: "I would contend that the workshop and its productions had a small number of critics within the SMA, on cultural, theological grounds. There were also a handful of enthusiasts for the workshop on the same grounds. The majority of the men were indifferent. On a leadership level there were mixed feelings. With the departure of Dr. Kelly from office the scheme was deprived of a major supporter. The incoming administration and some of the missionary bishops felt that it was costing too much. There was a feeling that the money could be better spent in building churches and schools, teacher training colleges, clinics. On a leadership level there seems to have been objections on the financial and pastoral level, rather than on the cultural or theological levels. Kevin Carroll was a frequent contributor to the Province's official magazine, *The African Missionary*. This magazine was vetted by the Administration before publication. His articles, many of them relating

to African Christian art, were approved by the same Provincial under whose leadership the scheme was closed. The principal reason for that closure seems to have been the financial cost and complaints from some bishops that other branches of the apostolate were losing out."

6. Observation by the SMA archivist: "Within a few years of the closure of the scheme SMA missionaries increasingly were calling on Carroll for advice on architecture and furnishing when building new churches. He was highly respected by the vast majority of the confreres. In my view 'missionary attitudes' were far more nuanced than that proposed by cultural anthropologists and historians. In fact the idea that the missionaries came in and imposed Western values is patronizing of existing Africa, portraying African culture/religions as weak and capably of being 'colonized.' Many elements of African culture and religion were robust. Africa took from western culture and religion what it required, no more and no less." See Edmund Hogan's article in *African Ecclesial Review* 24, no. 2 (April 1982), 71–80.

7. Borghero 2002.

8. Onobrakpeya 1992, 175.

REFERENCES

Bailey, Gauvin Alexander. 1999. *Art on the Jesuit Missions in Asia and Latin America, 1542–1773.* Toronto: University of Toronto Press.

Barrett, David B., and Todd M. Johnson. 2004. "Annual Statistical Table on Global Mission." *International Bulletin of Missionary Research.*

Beier, Ulli. 1957. *Sacred Wood Carvings.* Lagos: Special Publication, *Nigeria Magazine.*

———. 1960. *Art in Nigeria 1960.* Cambridge: Cambridge University Press.

———. 1968. *Contemporary Art in Africa.* New York: Frederick A. Praeger.

Borghero, Francesco. 2002. *Diario del Primo Missionario del Dahomey, 1860–1864*, edited by Renzo Mandirola. Bologna, Italy: Editrice Missionaria Italiana.

Bridger, Nicholas James. 2002. "The Oye-Ekiti Workshop and Its Origins: A Study of Missionary Art Patronage in Colonial Nigeria, 1947–1954." Master's thesis, San Francisco State University.

———. 2007. "Une Expression du Christianisme dans l'art du Nigeria: Kevin Carroll et l'Atelier d'Oye-Ekiti." *Histoire et Missions Chrétiennes*, no. 2 (June).

———. 2009. "Oye-Ekiti Workshop: Creating African Christian Art in Nigeria." *Material Religion* 5, no. 1 (March).

———. 2009. "L'arte cristiana yoruba, evoluzione di uno stile." *Afriche un Continente Tante Culture*, no. 84: 12–25.

———. 2009. "The Rediscovery of Religion in Contemporary Nigerian Art History." *Critical Interventions*, nos. 3–4 (Spring): 160–175.

Bruzzichelli, Pia, ed. 1963. *Arte Africa e Cristo.* Assisi, Italy: Pro Civitate Christiana.

Carroll, Kevin. 1950. "Yoruba Craft Work at Oye-Ekiti, Ondo Diocese." *Nigeria Magazine* 35: 344–354.

———. 1958. "Christian Art in Nigeria." *Liturgical Arts* 26, no. 3: 91–94.

———. 1959. "The Carved Door in the Catholic University Chapel." *Ibadan*, no. 5: 1–2.

———. 1966. Letter to John Picton, July 7. Kevin Carroll Collection, Archive, Irish Province of the Society of African Missions, Cork, Ireland.

———. 1967. *Yoruba Religious Carving, Pagan and Christian Sculpture in Nigeria and Dahomey.* London: Geoffrey Chapman.

———. 1969. "Diary, 1946–1969." Unpublished manuscript. Kevin Carroll Collection, Archive, Irish Province of the Society of African Missions, Cork, Ireland.

———. 1978. "Yoruba Sacred Carving." Typed draft article. Kevin Carroll Collection, Archive, Irish Province of the Society of African Missions, Cork, Ireland .

———. 1981. "Nigerian Christian Architecture." Typed draft manuscript. Kevin Carroll Collection, Archive, Irish Province of the Society of African Missions, Cork, Ireland.

———. 1982. "The Oye-Ekiti Scheme, 1946–1954." Photocopy of typed manuscript. Kevin Carroll Collection, Archive, Irish Province of the Society of African Missions, Cork, Ireland.

———. 1991. "Chapels in North Borgu." Typed unpublished manuscript. Kevin Carroll Collection, Archive, Irish Province of the Society of African Missions, Cork, Ireland.

———. 1992. *Architectures of Nigeria, Architectures of the Hausa and Yoruba Peoples and of the Many Peoples Between—Tradition and Modernization.* London: Ethnographica and the Society for African Missions (SMA).

Clark, John. 1998. *Modern Asian Art.* Honolulu: University of Hawaii Press.

Costantini, Celso. 1940. *L'Arte Cristiana nelle Missione: Manuale d'Arte Per I Missionari.* Rome: Urbaniana, Tipografia Poliglotta Vaticana.

———. 1944. *Dio Nascosto, Splendori di Fede e d'Arte nella Santa Eucarestia.* Rome: Tumminelli Editore, Roma Citta Universitaria.

Day, Patrick A. E. 1999. "Recent Wood Carving in Ibadan: Some Observations." *Nigerian Field* 64 (April): 3–27.

"Decree on the Missionary Activity of the Church." 1966. In *The Documents of Vatican II*, ed. Walter M. Abbott, 584–613. New York: The America Press.

Ekechukwu, A. U. 1988. "Theology of Religions and the Theological Problematic of Inculturation." In *Religion and African Culture: Inculturation—A Nigerian Perspective*, ed. A. U. Ekechukwu, 125–145. London: Spiritan Publications.

Fagg, William Buller. 1969. "The African Artist." In *Tradition and Creativity in Tribal Art*, ed. D. Biebuyck, 42–57. Berkeley: University of California Press.

Fakeye, Lamidi O., and Bruce Haight with David Curl. 1996. *Lamidi Olonade Fakeye: A Retrospective Exhibition and Autobiography.* Holland, MI: DePree Art Center and Gallery, Hope College.

Falola, Toyin. 2005. Introduction to *Christianity and Social Change in Africa: Essays in Honor of J. D. Y. Peel*, ed. Toyin Falola. Durham, NC: Carolina Academic Press.

Henze, Anton, and Theodor Filthaut. 1956. *Contemporary Church Art.* New York: Sheed and Ward.

Hogan, Edmund M. 1990. *The Irish Missionary Movement, A Historical Survey, 1830–1980*. Dublin: Gill and Macmillan.

jegede, dele. 1984. "Patronage and Change in Nigerian Art." *Nigeria Magazine*, no. 150: 29–36.

———.1990. "African Art Today, A Historical Overview." In *New York, The Studio Museum in Harlem*, 29–43.

Jenkins, Phillip. 2002. *The Next Christendom: The Coming of Global Christianity*. Oxford: Oxford University Press.

Kasfir, Sidney Littlefield. 1987. "Apprentices and Entrepreneurs: The Workshop and Style Uniformity in Subsaharan Africa." In *Iowa Studies in African Art*, ed. Christopher Roy, vol. 2, 25–47. Iowa City: University of Iowa.

———.1999. *Contemporary African Art*. London: Thames and Hudson.

Kelly, Patrick Martin. 1947. *Kindly Light, Being Educational Hopes of the S.M.A. in Africa*. Cork, Ireland: The African Missions.

———. 1950. "Notes." Typed manuscript. Archive, Society of African Missions, Irish Province, Cork, Ireland.

Kirby, Jon P. 1994. "Cultural Change and Religious Conversion in West Africa." In *Religion in Africa*, ed. Thomas D. Blakely et al., 56–71. Portsmouth, NH: Heineman.

Koenig, Robert J. n.d. "The African Art Museum of the SMA Fathers." In *The African Art Museum of the Society of African Missions at Tenafly: A Bridge between Cultures and Peoples*. Tenafly, NJ: African Art Museum of the SMA Fathers.

Lawal, Babatunde. 1977. *The Study of Contemporary Art in Nigeria: Towards a New Theoretical Framework*. Baltimore, MD: Thirty-third Annual Meeting of the African Studies Association.

Lugira, A.M.S. 1962. "Christ in African Art." *African Ecclesiastical Review* 4, no. 2: 127–134.

Miles, Elza. 2004. *Polly Street: The Story of an Art Centre*. Johannesburg, South Africa: Ampersand Foundation.

Mount, Marshall Ward. 1973. *African Art, the Years since 1920*. Bloomington: Indiana University Press.

O'Brien, Joanne, and Martin Palmer. 2007. *The Atlas of Religion*. Berkeley: University of California Press.

Ojo, Joseph Bayode. 1993. "Songs of Praise at the Funeral Mass of Kevin Carroll, SMA." Translated by anonymous. Photocopied text. Kevin Carroll Collection, Archive, Irish Province of the Society of African Missions, Cork, Ireland.

Okeke, Uche. 1979. "History of Modern Nigerian Art." *Nigeria Magazine*, nos. 128–129: 100–118.

Onobrakpeya, Bruce. 1970. *Ki Ijoba Re De* [Thy Kingdom Come]. Catholic Secretariat of Nigeria, 1969. Reprint. London: Geoffrey Chapman.

———. 1992. *Bruce Onobrakpeya: The Spirit in Ascent*. Lagos, Nigeria: Ovuomarroro Gallery.

Ostling, Richard N. 1989. "Christian Art in Africa." *Time* (March 27), 76–79.

Peel, J.D.Y. 1989. "The Cultural Work of Yoruba Ethnogenesis." In *History and*

Ethnicity, ed. Elizabeth Tonkin, Maryon MacDonald, and Malcolm Chapman, 198–215. London: Routledge.

———. 2000. *Religious Encounter and the Making of the Yoruba.* Bloomington: University of Indiana Press.

Perani, Judith. 1997. Review of "Lamidi Olonade Fakeye: A Retrospective Exhibition." *African Arts* 30, no. 4: 79–81.

Picton, John. 1994a. "Art, Identity and Identification: A Commentary on Yoruba Art Historical Studies." In *The Yoruba Artist*, ed. Rowland Abiodun, Henry John Drewal, and John Pemberton III, 1–34. Washington, DC: Smithsonian Institution Press.

———. 1994b. "In Memoriam: Father Kevin Caroll, SMA." *African Arts* 27, no. 3: 25, 98.

———. 1994c. "Sculptors of Opin." *African Arts* 27, no. 3: 46–59, 101–102.

———. 2002. "Neo-Traditional Sculpture in Nigeria." In *An Anthology of African Art: The Twentieth Century*, ed. N'Gone Falls and Jean Loup Pivin, 100–101. New York: Distributed Art Publishers.

———. 2004. "On Marking and Masking in the Art of Bruce Onobrakpeya." In *Where Gods and Mortals Meet: Continuity and Renewal in Urhobo Art*, ed. Perkins Foss, 131–133. New York: Museum for African Art.

Satolli, Dino. 1952. *Exposicao De Arte Sacra Missionaria, A Exposicao dos Jeronimos.* Translated by Melina Mattos. Lisbon: Agencia Geral do Ultramar.

SMA. 1993. Kevin Francis Carroll Obituary, 1993. Kevin Carroll Collection, Archive, Irish Province of the Society of African Missions, Cork, Ireland.

Stanley, Brian. 2003. Introduction to *Christianity and the End of Empire.* Cambridge: William B. Eerdmans Publishing Company.

Thornton, John. 1984. "The development of an African Catholic church in the Kingdom of the Kongo, 1491–1750." *Journal of African History,* 25:147–167.

———. 1992. *Africa and Africans in the Making of the Atlantic World, 1400–1800.* Cambridge: Cambridge University Press.

Visona, Monica Blackmun, Robyn Poynor, Herbert M. Cole, and Michael D. Harris. 2001. *A History of Art in Africa.* New York: Harry N. Abrams.

Walker, Roslyn. 1998. *Olowe of Ise, A Yoruba Sculptor to Kings.* Washington, DC: National Museum of African Art, Smithsonian Institution.

Walls, Andrew F. 1996. The *Missionary Movement in Christian History: Studies in the Transmission of Faith.* Maryknoll, NY: Orbis Books.

———. 2002. *The Cross-Cultural Process in Christian History: Studies in the Transmission and Appropriation of Faith.* Maryknoll, NY: Orbis Books.

Willett, Frank. 1960. "Introduction." In *The Sculpture of Western Nigeria*. Ibadan, Nigeria: Ministry of Western Nigeria.

Willet, Frank. 1971. *African Art.* London: Thames and Hudson.

INDEX